Our E

Huma.. World

2024 Edition

JJ Kinkaid

Explore Time, Space, our Earth and Moon, our waters and soils, our bodies, and our ancestors, and embrace the ingenuity of humanity. Celebrate Our Exquisitely Human World! Even a tiny change in the Oxygen available or the Earth's gravity or just a bit closer to or further away from the sun ... we wouldn't be here. It's as if this universe were designed just for us. Let's rejoice!

"Judge each day not by the harvest you reap but by the seeds you plant."
~Robert Louis Stevenson

Time

Fun Facts

Time's Gravity Waltz: Did you know that time dances differently depending on where you are? Thanks to Einstein's theory of relativity, time actually passes faster for your face than your feet if you're standing up! It's true – closer to Earth's center, time slows down. Imagine celebrating New Year's Eve on Mount Everest – your year would be 15 microseconds shorter than if you were at sea level!

A Second, Redefined: Forget the old 1/60th of a minute; a second in the scientific world is defined by cesium atoms. It's precisely 9,192,631,770 periods of radiation transitions in cesium 133 atoms. A tiny atomic tick-tock setting the pace for our entire world.

The Earth's Speedy Spin: Earth's daily spin isn't a perfect 24 hours but 23 hours, 56 minutes, and 4.2 seconds. Why? As Earth orbits the sun, its position changes slightly, extending our experience of a day. It's like the Earth is sneaking in a few extra moments under the sun.

Dinosaur Days and Lengthening Years: When dinosaurs roamed, a year had 370 days! Earth's spin is slowing down, thanks to the moon's gravitational tug. This celestial dance is adding about 1.7 milliseconds to our days every century.

Blink in a Planck: The smallest standard scientific measure of time is the Planck time. To put it in perspective, blinking quickly takes you about 550 quintillion quintillion quintillion Planck times. Or 550,000,000,000,000,000,000,000,000,000,000,000,000,000,00 0,000,000,000,000 Planck times!

Ancient Timekeepers: Marking time is as old as civilization. The Sumerians and Egyptians used sundials around 1500 BC, creating the early shadows of timekeeping.

Caesar's Calendar Correction: Julius Caesar was more than a ruler; he was a calendar innovator. In 46 BC, he introduced the leap year to align the calendar with the solar year. A timely adjustment, indeed!

The Puzzle of Time Dilation: Time dilation is a relative phenomenon. It means that time can pass at different rates for different observers, either due to their relative velocity or differences in gravitational potential. It's like you have your own unique time bubble!

The Date Line Divide: The International Date Line isn't just a figment of our imaginations. It's an invisible line from the North to the South Pole, marking where one-day ends and the next begins. A true divider of today and tomorrow.

Space-Time for GPS: GPS technology has to consider time dilation. Time ticks faster in space than on Earth, so our global positioning friends in the sky need a bit of temporal tuning to keep us on the right track.

The Atomic Clock's Precision: The atomic clock is a master of time, losing only about one second every 100 million years. It's like the Swiss watch of the quantum world.

China's Ancient Chronicles: The Chinese were timekeeping trailblazers, recording events in yearly cycles from as early as 2637 BC. Talk about a long-term planner!

Egypt's Time-Tested Sundial: The oldest known sundial dates back to at least the 8th Century BC in Egypt. It's not just an artifact; it's a shadow-casting timepiece of ancient wisdom.

Hourglass: Time's Sand Dancer: Before digital clocks, there was the humble hourglass, dating back to the 14th century. Sands of time, literally falling through history.

Gravity's Taffy Time: Scientists have shown that gravity can stretch time, just like taffy. Using a new atomic clock, they've measured time slowing down over a mere millimeter – proving that even the smallest distances can have a big impact on time.

The Most Popular Word: "Time" isn't just a concept; it's the most used noun in the English language. It seems we're all a bit obsessed with time, aren't we?

A Jiffy, in a Jiffy: A 'jiffy' is more than just quick; it's precisely 1/100th of a second. So next time someone says, "I'll be there in a jiffy," you'll know they are serious.

Living in the Past: Technically, we all live a tiny bit in the past. Our brains take about 80 milliseconds to process events, meaning we're always playing a slight catch-up with reality. "Now" is more of a charming illusion than a pinpoint in time.

The Moon's Slow Dance: The moon isn't just Earth's companion; it's also slowing our spin. Tidal braking, thanks to the moon's pull, adds 2.3 milliseconds to our days every century.

Attoseconds and Quantum Leaps: An attosecond is unimaginably brief – a quintillionth of a second. In 2023, physicists Anne L'Huillier, Pierre Agostini, and Ferenc Krausz were awarded the Nobel Prize for creating attosecond pulses of light, a monumental leap in studying electron dynamics.

A Galactic Ballet

Embark on an enchanting odyssey through the mysteries of time, starting with our very own Earth. Here, time pirouettes to the rhythm of Earth's twirls and spins. From ancient sundials to the modern marvels of atomic clocks, our journey of timekeeping is nothing short of magical. These atomic timekeepers, precise to an almost fantastical degree, lose barely a second over a million years. Our daily lives are choreographed by Earth's celestial dance – a day marked by a single spin, a year by a grand orbit around the sun. It's a cosmic routine that has set the stage for human existence.

Sir Isaac Newton envisioned time as a steadfast arrow, unswerving and unwavering, cutting through the cosmos. Newton's time was absolute, unchanging from Earth to the furthest star, presenting us with a universe of comforting predictability and uniformity.

But the narrative takes a thrilling twist with Albert Einstein's groundbreaking Theory of Relativity. Here, time transforms from Newton's unyielding arrow into a fluid, dynamic river. Einstein's universe is a stage where time dances to the gravitational pull, slowing and quickening in a mesmerizing waltz that varies with velocity and mass. This revelation of time dilation turned our understanding on its head, painting time as a malleable participant in the cosmic ballet.

This revelation propels us into the starlit vastness of space, where time and distance intertwine elegantly. The concept of light-years turns our stargazing into time-traveling escapades. As we gaze at stars and galaxies millions of light-years away, we're actually spectators to a historical cosmic show, witnessing these celestial bodies as they were eons ago. It's like unearthing a galactic time capsule, each star a story from the universe's ancient past.

Delving into the quantum realm, we enter a domain where time, that ever familiar and linear companion of our everyday lives, begins to unveil its most enigmatic and enthralling characteristics. Here, beneath the surface of our macroscopic understanding, the rules of traditional physics give way to a world where time assumes a surreal duality. This is the realm of 'T-symmetry', a quantum phenomenon where time exhibits a remarkable flexibility, flowing both forwards and backwards.

In classical physics, time is a one-way street, always marching forward, but in the quantum world, it's more like a bidirectional highway. T-symmetry, short for time-reversal symmetry, implies that certain physical processes can occur in reverse without violating the fundamental laws of physics. This doesn't mean we can reverse time as we experience it, but rather, at the quantum level, particles can follow the same rules whether time is moving forwards or backwards. It's as if you could run a film of a quantum event in reverse, and it would still make perfect sense within the quantum realm. Much like a palindrome: noon, kayak, or radar.

Adding to the quantum tapestry is the revolutionary concept of 'Time Crystals'. These extraordinary structures organize themselves into a repeating pattern in motion rather than space. We may like to think orbits are consistently elliptical, but in reality, planets, stars and other objects are being pulled in many directions. The Universe tends toward disorder over time. Time Crystals can negate that entropy ... as long as we're not looking at them. Upon observation, the quantum system collapses. Quantum systems are a lot like a toddler putting away toys in his room without being asked. He's happy to do it as long as no one is watching. Upon observation the task shifts from joy to a chore with maximum resistance.

What's intriguing about Time Crystals is that they are in perpetual motion without energy input, a state that seems to defy the traditional laws of thermodynamics. This perpetual oscillation occurs at the quantum level, where the usual rules of energy and motion don't apply in the same way as they do in our everyday experience. Time Crystals maintain their temporal structure despite external fluctuations, showcasing a regular, clock-like ticking at their core, independent of their surroundings.

This quantum realm invites us to rethink time, not as a simple, unidirectional flow, but as a rich, complex, and deeply intertwined element of the universe's foundation, a vibrant and mysterious phenomenon that continues to captivate and puzzle scientists.

Outrageous Ideas

Time's Consciousness: The Sentient Dimension

Have you ever considered the possibility that time itself might possess a form of consciousness? This mesmerizing concept emerges from the intriguing crossroads of quantum mechanics and consciousness studies. Just as quantum particles behave differently under observation, could time, interlaced with the fabric of the universe, hold its own awareness? This theory, as enchanting as it is profound, suggests that time might be more than a passive dimension; it could be an active, shaping force in the cosmos, an unseen artist painting the strokes of reality.

The Multidimensional Time Maze: Exploring Time's Hidden Pathways

Venture into a universe where time is not a single, linear river but a labyrinth of countless dimensions. Inspired by the bewildering many-worlds interpretation of quantum mechanics, this concept proposes a universe where parallel timelines exist, similar to the multiple directions in space. Imagine a world where each decision creates a new path in time, where every moment branches into an infinite array of futures. This fantastical idea expands our understanding of time, transforming it from a singular path to a grand, multidimensional tapestry.

Quantum Time Shards: The Multiverse Mosaic, A Universe of Infinite Possibilities

Enter the realm of quantum time shards, where time fractures into countless fragments at the quantum level. Each decision, each quantum event, shatters the moment into a myriad of parallel realities, creating a kaleidoscope of possible histories and futures. This theory, emerging from the depths of quantum mechanics, suggests that what we perceive as a continuous flow of time might actually be a complex mosaic of temporal fragments, each a doorway to a different universe within the quantum foam.

Time as a Living Tapestry: The Evolving Pulse of the Cosmos

Imagine time not as an inanimate dimension, but as a living, evolving entity. Drawing from the captivating theories of biocentrism, this idea envisions time as a dynamic organism, growing and adapting in response to the universe's rhythms. Just as living creatures evolve, so too could time, changing and developing new characteristics. In this enthralling perspective, time becomes a living part of the cosmos, a dynamic participant in the eternal dance of existence.

Retrocausality: Echoes from the Future

Step into the enigmatic world of retrocausality, where the future can reach back to whisper to the past. Grounded in the peculiarities of quantum mechanics, this concept turns our traditional understanding of cause and effect on its head. What if choices made in the future could influence events that have already happened? This mesmerizing idea suggests a universe where time loops and intertwines, allowing for the possibility of time travel and messages from the future altering the course of history.

Space

Imagination will often carry us to worlds that never were. But without it, we go nowhere."
~Carl Sagan

Fun Facts

Twinkling Stars Aren't Just Twinkling: When you gaze up at the night sky, the twinkling stars are actually not twinkling. This effect is caused by Earth's atmosphere distorting the light from these distant suns. In space, stars shine steadily!

Diamond Planets Exist: Imagine a planet made almost entirely of diamond! Such an exotic world exists. Named 55 Cancri e, this planet's mass is thought to be one-third pure diamond, a result of its carbon-rich composition under extreme pressure. A cosmic jeweler's dream!

A Colossal Water Reservoir in Space: Floating in space is a massive cloud of vapor containing 140 trillion times the amount of water in Earth's oceans. This cloud surrounds a quasar located 12 billion light-years away.

Galaxies in Collision: Our Milky Way galaxy is on a collision course with the Andromeda galaxy. Fear not, this event is set to occur in about 4 billion years, and given the vast distances between stars, it's unlikely any stars will actually collide.

A Planet of Burning Ice: There's a planet, known as Gliese 436 b, where the temperatures reach a scorching 822°F (439°C), yet it is covered in ice. The gravity is so strong that it compresses the water vapor into solid ice despite the high temperatures.

The Largest Known Structure in the Universe: The Hercules-Corona Borealis Great Wall, a gigantic galactic supercluster, is the largest known structure in the universe. It stretches over 10 billion light-years!

A Planet with Iron Rain: WASP-76b is a bizarre world where temperatures reach 4,300°F (2,400°C) during the day, hot enough to vaporize metals. At night, temperatures drop, causing iron rain.

Oldest Known Star: The star SMSS J031300.36-670839.3 is about 13.6 billion years old, nearly as old as the universe itself. It's a real cosmic relic, having formed shortly after the Big Bang.

The Color of the Universe: The average color of the universe is a beige-like shade. Astronomers playfully named it "Cosmic Latte." This color represents the average light emission from the diverse galaxies and stars.

A Year Lasting Only 8.5 Hours: On the exoplanet PSR J1719-1438 b, a year, or one orbit around its star, takes only 8.5 hours. The planet's proximity to its star results in incredibly rapid orbital speed.

Space's Silent Symphony: Space might seem silent, but it's filled with "sounds." Astronomers convert radio emissions and plasma waves into sound waves, unveiling the hidden symphony of planets, stars, and galaxies.

A Ghostly Green Nebula: The Ghost Nebula, ethereal and haunting, is a cloud of gas and dust illuminated by the nearby stars. Its greenish hue comes from doubly ionized oxygen.

Rogue Planets Roaming Free: Some planets don't orbit any star. These rogue or orphan planets drift through the galaxy, untethered to a solar system.

A Star Older Than the Universe?: Methuselah Star, or HD 140283, seemed to pose a cosmic paradox. Initial measurements suggested it was older than the universe! Revised estimates now place it just slightly younger, highlighting the complexities of cosmic measurement.

The Never-Ending Echo of the Big Bang: The Cosmic Microwave Background is the afterglow of the Big Bang, still detectable as a faint microwave signal enveloping the universe. It's like seeing the universe's 380,000 year baby photo!

The Great Wall of Galaxies: The Sloan Great Wall, a giant wall of galaxies, measures over 1.37 billion light-years in length, making it one of the largest known cosmic structures.

Black Hole's Shadow Captured: In 2019, astronomers captured the first image of a black hole's shadow, a historic achievement that provided visual evidence of these mysterious entities.

Stars That Sing: Some stars have been found to produce sound waves. While not audible in space, these vibrations can be detected by instruments, revealing insights into the star's interior.

The Dancing Galaxies of Stephan's Quintet: Stephan's Quintet, a group of five galaxies, is known for its complex gravitational interactions, causing a cosmic dance of epic proportions.

Dark Matter Bridges: Astronomers have detected invisible 'bridges' of dark matter linking galaxy clusters, providing critical clues about the universe's structure and evolution.

Sagittarius B's Intoxicating Cloud: In the constellation of Sagittarius B, there's a cloud of alcohol so vast it's a thousand times the diameter of our solar system. The universe's own distillery!

Shooting Stars: A Misnomer: Those streaks of light in the night sky, called shooting stars, are actually meteors – small bits of cosmic dust igniting in Earth's atmosphere.

The Star-Studded Sky: The universe is a grand stage, with more stars than all the grains of sand on Earth's beaches – that's at least a billion trillion! A cosmic extravaganza beyond measure.

Earth's Twin Discovered by Webb Telescope: The James Webb Space Telescope has unveiled a cosmic twin to our home planet!

Meet LHS 475 b, an exoplanet almost mirroring Earth, at 99% of our planet's diameter. This rocky neighbor was spotted thanks to the sharp eyes of NASA's Transiting Exoplanet Survey Satellite (TESS) and confirmed by Webb's Near-Infrared Spectrograph.

Hycean World: A "Hycean" world is a type of exoplanet that has been hypothesized by astronomers as a potential candidate for hosting alien life. These planets are characterized by their hydrogen-rich atmospheres and are thought to be covered by wide, deep oceans. The term "Hycean" combines aspects of both hydrogen and ocean.

K2-18 b, Hycean?: Another great find, the James Webb Space Telescope has unraveled the secrets of K2-18 b, an exoplanet over 8 times Earth's mass. This celestial body is stirring excitement with signs of carbon-rich molecules like methane and carbon dioxide. But here's the kicker – it might be a Hycean world. Intriguingly, it even shows hints of dimethyl sulfide, a molecule associated with life on Earth, particularly marine phytoplankton. K2-18 b stands as a beacon in our quest to understand life-sustaining exoplanets.

Rain of Sand on WASP-107b: In a revelation straight out of a sci-fi novel, the James Webb Space Telescope has discovered that the Neptune-like exoplanet WASP-107b, residing 211 light-years away, experiences something out of this world – sand rain! Its atmosphere, rich with water vapor and sulfur dioxide, features clouds made of silicates that form raindrops of sand.

How Big is the Universe?

Imagine a cozy room with a bunch of playful puppies – a scene brimming with joy and easy to cherish. It seems absurd to even say it, but surely you could tell the difference between 8 puppies and 16 puppies. Now, envision that number increasing. The room transforms into a bustling whirlwind of wagging tails and barks. Can you distinguish between 80 puppies and 160 puppies? Maybe. Escalate this further, and you're suddenly overwhelmed by an unimaginable wave of furry friends! Can you tell the difference between 800 puppies and 1600 puppies in the room? Most of us cannot. Once we are unable to physically count the puppies in front of us, the number becomes an abstraction. Our brain no longer values counting precisely, an approximation will do.

This leap from the manageable to the overwhelming exemplifies the concept of 'order of magnitude', a tool that helps us comprehend the staggering scale of the universe. Rather than get bogged down with precision, 812 puppies for example, we focus on the accurate order of magnitude, approximately 1000 puppies. One-thousand puppies puts you in the accurate range, 800 to 1600 for example, before you bog down with the precise number.

An order-of-magnitude estimate of a variable, whose precise value is unknown, is an estimate rounded to the nearest power of ten. For example, an order-of-magnitude estimate for a variable between about 3 billion and 30 billion (such as the human population of the Earth) is 10 billion; 1 billion is too low and 100 billion is too high. Ten billion is a decent placeholder.

The Universe, as we understand it, is a breathtakingly vast and complex entity, encompassing everything that exists from the tiniest particles to the grandest galaxies: the entirety of space and time. It is a wondrous expanse estimated to be 13.8 billion years old, a number so large it's like counting every grain of sand on all of Earth's beaches. This estimate comes from the Lambda cold dark matter model, the most widely accepted cosmological model. Lambda-CDM states that the Universe started with a singularity event known as the Big Bang, and it's been expanding ever since.

Ordinary matter, which includes stars, planets, galaxies, and everything that we can see or touch, surprisingly only makes up about 5% of the Universe. This 'ordinary matter' is akin to the sprinkling of glitter on a vast, dark canvas – it's what forms the visible and tangible structures in the universe, the stuff of atoms and molecules, yet it plays a minor role in the universe's grand composition.

The current accepted theory is that the other 95% is made up of mysterious entities: dark matter and dark energy. Dark matter, a non-luminous material that doesn't interact with electromagnetic force is thought to make up about 27% of the Universe. It can't be directly observed, but its existence is inferred through its gravitational effects on visible matter. This means it doesn't absorb, reflect, or emit light, making it incredibly difficult to spot. Dark energy, accounting for approximately 68%, is even more elusive. It is thought to be driving the accelerated expansion of the Universe, a phenomenon discovered in the late 20th century.

Dark matter, making up about 27% of the universe, is like the invisible scaffolding of a massive building. Just as the scaffolding supports and shapes a building even though it's not immediately visible, dark matter forms the unseen structure that holds galaxies together. It's like trying to understand the outline of a dark room; you can't see the walls, but you believe they're there because they define the space.

Introducing Weakly Interacting Massive Particles, or WIMPs – the universe's elusive specters. These hypothetical particles, which could be the core of dark matter, are ghostly dancers in the cosmic saga. They interact so faintly through gravity and the weak nuclear force that catching a glimpse of them is a monumental challenge. WIMPs are thought to be relics from the universe's infancy, potential "thermal relics". WIMP models are attractive because they naturally arise in supersymmetry theories to address the short comings of particle physics.

Now, for a twist in our cosmic tale: what if dark matter is merely an illusion, a cosmic mirage? Modified Newtonian Dynamics (MOND) presents a bold and somewhat rebellious theory, suggesting that maybe our understanding of gravity needs a rewrite. MOND proposes that the laws governing gravity's pull might dance to a different tune across the vast expanse of space. Much in the same vein as the way time varies across space. What if the inconsistencies in galactic rotations, which the existence of dark matter explains, are due to a modification in Newton's laws at extremely low accelerations, removing the need for dark matter?

Then the Big Bang theory falls apart.

Another controversial theory, the Plasma Universe theory, also challenges the mainstream view. Proponents of this theory argue that electromagnetic processes, not gravity, play the main role in the Universe's large-scale structure formation. This theory emphasizes the importance of plasma—ionized gas with equal numbers of positive and negative charges—in cosmic physics. It would be more akin to building buildings with the invisible energy between molecules like in the human body than steel.

At an atomic level, the human body is predominantly made up of empty space. When we look at an atom, which is the basic building block of matter, it consists of a nucleus (comprising protons and neutrons) and electrons that orbit this nucleus. The surprising fact is that these particles are incredibly tiny and the distances between them are relatively vast.

To give a more concrete perspective, if you consider the nucleus of an atom as a marble and place it in the center of a large sports stadium, the electrons would be like tiny peas whizzing around in the furthest reaches of the stands. The rest of the stadium, which represents the majority of the atom's volume, is empty space.

Thus, if we could somehow remove all the empty space from the atoms making up a human body, the actual matter would condense to an incredibly small volume. However, it's important to understand that this "empty space" isn't truly empty; it is filled with various fields and forces that define the behavior of these atoms and, consequently, the matter that we interact with in our daily lives. This concept is counterintuitive because the forces at play within this space (like electromagnetic forces) make matter appear solid and tangible at our scale of perception.

The Universe has very little ordinary matter much like the human body. A plasma source is directly converted into electrical energy without the use of any mechanical energy very efficiently. If the plasma theory holds, the Universe is held together by electromagnetic forces rather than WIMPs. It may indicate that the Universe had no beginning and has no end. Critics claim the Plasma Universe ended about 380,000 years after the Big Bang. And are quick to remind, that though concepts of plasma can be executed in the lab, it may be too bold to extrapolate the theory to the Universe.

It is worth noting that the true nature of dark matter might be something entirely different from these theories. The search for dark matter continues to be one of the most exciting and challenging quests in cosmology.

Dark energy, representing around 68% of the Universe, is even more mysterious. It's a form of energy causing the Universe's accelerated expansion. However, our understanding of it remains rudimentary at best, with the exact properties and nature of dark energy still unknown. Dark energy is a hypothetical form of energy that permeates all space and accelerates the expansion of the Universe. It was first postulated in the late 20th century when observations of distant supernovae suggested that the Universe's expansion was accelerating rather than slowing down as previously thought. Dark energy is like a mysterious force behind a curtain, constantly pushing the fabric of space to expand. Imagine blowing up a balloon with tiny dots on it. As the balloon inflates, the dots move farther apart – this is similar to how galaxies move away from each other in our expanding universe. Dark energy is the unseen breath that keeps inflating the cosmic balloon, a force that's everywhere but remains unseen and elusive.

Albert Einstein first introduced the cosmological constant in 1917. Picture this as a sprinkle of cosmic dust that fills space evenly, a uniform energy density that fills space homogeneously and does not dilute as the Universe expands. However, it was initially conceived as a "fudge factor" by Einstein to allow a static Universe solution in his General Theory of Relativity. He later abandoned the idea when the Universe was found to be expanding, but the concept was revived in the context of dark energy.

Another crucial element in our understanding of the Universe's nature is the Hubble constant, a measure of the Universe's expansion rate. Named after the American astronomer Edwin Hubble, the constant helps determine the age and size of the Universe. However, there's an ongoing debate known as the "Hubble Tension." Different methods of measuring the Hubble constant yield different results. For instance, measurements from the cosmic microwave background radiation suggest a slower expansion rate than those from distance ladder methods that use variable stars and supernovae. In other words, we can't even agree on how to measure it!

In the most intriguing chapter yet, some scientists ponder if dark energy is a signal that we need to venture beyond Einstein's playbook. Could there be new, unseen particles or perhaps a twist in the tale of gravity itself? This theory is like peering through a telescope into uncharted territories of the universe, hinting at undiscovered wonders and profound new physics waiting to be revealed.

Imagine this: a field that changes its energy density over time and space, painting the cosmos with varying strokes. Quintessence is not a fixed backdrop; it's an active player, sometimes pulling objects together, other times pushing them apart. It's a concept that adds a dash of dynamism and mystery to our understanding of the universe, challenging us to rethink the very fabric of cosmic reality. It is yet another attempt to reconcile the expanding universe with our limited understanding of the forces at play!

Outrageous Ideas

Venturing beyond the confines of our known universe, we encounter the captivating and complex theory of multiverses. This concept isn't just a single idea but a tapestry of theories, each proposing a different type of universe existing beyond our own.

String theory, a candidate for the theory of everything, implies a vast landscape of possible universes within higher-dimensional space. These universes might have different dimensions or different constants of nature from our own. One prominent theory is the Bubble Universe theory, part of the eternal inflation model. It suggests that our universe is just one bubble in a frothy sea of universe bubbles, each formed during a period of rapid expansion and possibly featuring different physical laws. What goes up may not actually need to come down.

Another intriguing theory is the Quantum Multiverse, born from the interpretations of quantum mechanics. It posits that every decision or event creates a new universe, leading to an infinite branching of realities based on different outcomes. Imagine if every choice you've ever made – every left turn, every yes or no – spawned a new universe where you made a different choice. All possible alternate histories and futures are real and exist in parallel universes. This concept goes beyond science into the philosophical, raising questions about the nature of reality and our place in it. It is driven by events, choices.

While related to the Many-Worlds Interpretation or Quantum Multiverse, the Parallel Universes theory, proposes that universes run parallel to our own, perhaps just out of reach of our current observational capabilities - independent of choices. These universes could be incredibly similar to ours or vastly different. And they could occupy the same space. There could be infinite parallel versions of You occupying the space you are in right now. We can't see the space between atoms, but there is more open space within your atoms than there is material, much like the organization of the Universe.

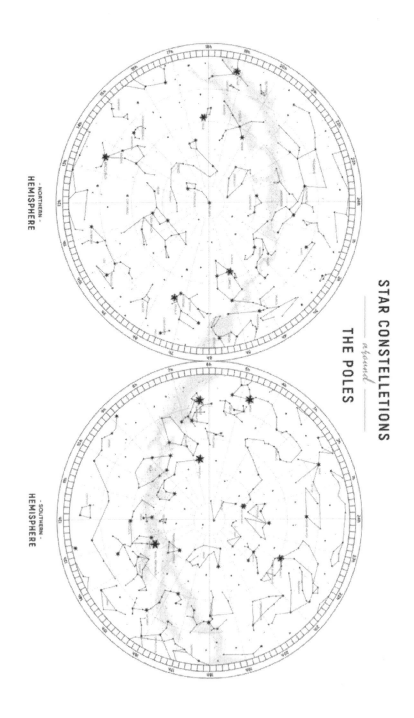

STAR CONSTELLETIONS
around
THE POLES

- NORTHERN -
HEMISPHERE

- SOUTHERN -
HEMISPHERE

Solar System

Fun Facts

Jupiter's Mighty Magnetic Field: Jupiter's magnetic field is a colossal force, 14 times stronger than Earth's. This immense field, the strongest of any planet in our solar system, extends millions of miles into space, acting like a giant cosmic shield against solar radiation.

Jupiter's Moon Ensemble: Jupiter isn't just the largest planet; it's also the king of moons in our solar system. With a staggering 79 known moons orbiting it, each moon offers a unique world to explore, from volcanic Io to ice-covered Europa.

Saturn's Floatability: Imagine a planet so light that it could float in water! That's Saturn for you. Despite its massive size, Saturn's density is less than that of water, making it the only planet in our solar system that could theoretically bob in an enormous cosmic ocean.

Uranus' Unique Tilt: Uranus stands out in the solar dance by spinning on its side. With an axial tilt of about 98 degrees, it's as if Uranus is rolling along its orbital path around the Sun, offering a unique perspective of its moons and rings.

Venus' Metallic Snow and Acid Rain: Venus, our neighboring planet, is a world of extremes. Its thick atmosphere and scorching temperatures lead to metallic snow and sulfuric acid rain, painting a picture of a harsh, alien world unlike any other in the solar system.

The Sun's Energetic Core: The heart of our solar system, the Sun, is a powerhouse of nuclear energy. Every second, its core releases energy equivalent to 100 billion nuclear bombs, fueling the Sun's heat and light that supports life on Earth.

Earth's Leisurely Spin: Our planet is taking its sweet time. Earth's rotation is gradually slowing down at a rate of about 17 milliseconds per hundred years. This means days are getting longer, but so gradually that it takes about 140 million years for our day to lengthen by just one hour.

Neptune's Mathematical Discovery: Neptune, a distant blue giant, was the first planet found using math, not direct observation. Astronomers used mathematical predictions to locate it, uncovering its existence through the gravitational pull it exerted on neighboring Uranus.

Haumea's Rapid Rotation: The dwarf planet Haumea, residing in the distant Kuiper belt, is a fast spinner. Shaped like a rugby ball due to its rapid rotation, it completes one full turn on its axis in just under 4 hours, making it one of the fastest rotating large objects in our solar system.

Mercury's Speedy Year: On Mercury, a year is a brief affair. Orbiting the Sun in just 88 Earth days, Mercury experiences the shortest year of all the planets in our solar system. This rapid orbit makes Mercury a fascinating study in extreme temperatures and solar influence.

Titan's Liquid Lakes: Saturn's moon Titan is an enigmatic world with its thick atmosphere and lakes of liquid methane and ethane. It's one of the few places, besides Earth, where we've found stable bodies of surface liquid, making it a prime target in the search for extraterrestrial life.

Mars' Temperature Highs: Mars, often thought of as a cold, desert world, can surprise us. At its equator, in the middle of the day, temperatures can soar up to 86°Fahrenheit, offering a more Earth-like condition than often imagined.

Enceladus' Water Geysers: Saturn's icy moon Enceladus hides a secret beneath its frozen surface. Geysers there shoot water vapor 124 miles (200 kilometers) into space, hinting at a subsurface ocean, making it a compelling location in the search for life beyond Earth.

The Sun's Near-Perfect Sphericity: Our Sun, a glowing orb at the center of our solar system, is an almost perfect sphere. The difference in its polar and equatorial diameters is a mere 6 miles (10 kilometers), a tiny variance for such a massive object.

Miranda's Geologic Patchwork: Uranus' moon Miranda presents a geological mystery. It appears to be a patchwork of varied terrains stitched together, featuring cliffs and valleys that tell a story of a complex and violent geological past.

Jupiter's Great Red Spot: The Great Red Spot on Jupiter is a gigantic storm, larger than three Earths combined, that has been swirling for over 300 years. This enduring storm offers scientists a window into Jupiter's atmospheric dynamics.

The Sun's Hot Corona: The Sun's outermost layer, the corona, is a puzzle. Despite being farther from the Sun's core, it's hotter than the surface, reaching temperatures millions of degrees hotter, a phenomenon that challenges our understanding of solar physics.

CORONA
CHROMOSPHERE
PHOTOSPHERE
CONVECTIVE ZONE
RADIATIVE ZONE
CORE

Fusion in the core where temperatures reach 15 million °C
Produces all the Sun's heat and light

Pluto's Heart of Ice: Pluto, once considered the ninth planet, features a distinct heart-shaped region called Tombaugh Regio. This area is covered in nitrogen ice and plays a key role in Pluto's climate and atmospheric patterns.

The Asteroid Belt's Diversity: The asteroid belt, located between Mars and Jupiter, is a cosmic repository of rock and metal. It's home to thousands of asteroids, including the dwarf planet Ceres, offering clues to the early solar system's formation.

Mars' Grand Canyon: Mars is home to Valles Marineris, a canyon system that dwarfs Earth's Grand Canyon. Stretching 2,500 miles (4,000 kilometers) long and reaching depths of over 4 miles (7 kilometers), it's a testament to the dynamic geological forces at work on the Red Planet.

Venus, the Surprising Scorcher: Mercury may be the Sun's nearest neighbor, but Venus, wrapped in its thick, heat-trapping atmosphere, reigns as the solar system's hottest planet. It's like a celestial sauna!

Mars' Skyward Giants: Mars boasts Olympus Mons, a colossal shield volcano, towering nearly three times higher than Mount Everest. A volcano so massive it could easily blanket the entire state of Arizona. It's the Martian mountain of legends!

Neptune's Furious Winds: On Neptune, hold onto your space hats! Here, winds whip through at a breathtaking 1,300 miles (2,100 kilometers) per hour, the fastest in the solar system.

Saturn's Lesser-Known Ringed Cousins: Saturn's not the only show-off with rings. Jupiter, Uranus, and Neptune each boast their own, albeit fainter, ring systems. A galactic trendsetter!

The Milky Way's Slow Dance: Our Milky Way galaxy is in a constant spin, traveling at a dizzying almost 500,000 miles per hour, yet it takes 220 million years to complete a single twirl.

The Sun's Mighty Mass: Our solar system's mass is overwhelmingly sun-centric, with this fiery giant holding 99.86% of the total. Truly, the sun is the cosmic heavyweight.

Inside the Sun's Fiery Heart: The core of the sun is an inferno beyond imagination, with temperatures soaring to a blistering 27 million degrees Fahrenheit (15 million degrees Celsius).

Venus' Ponderous Spin: A day on Venus outlasts its year, taking 243 Earth days to rotate just once, while its year is a shorter 225 Earth days. A planet that likes to take its time.

Ganymede's Deep Blue Secrets: Jupiter's moon, Ganymede, harbors the solar system's deepest ocean, a hidden world of water estimated to be 500 miles (800 kilometers deep), 10 times the depth of Earth's oceans.

Pluto's Small Stature: Tiny Pluto, a dwarf planet, is so petite that it's smaller than the United States in width. A small world with a big heart.

Space's No-Burp Zone: In the weightlessness of space, astronauts find they can't burp – gravity can't separate the gas from liquids in their stomachs.

The Asteroid Belt's Light Touch: The asteroid belt, a cosmic scattering of rocks, is only 5% as massive as our moon. A lightweight in the planetary ring.

Vesta's Mountainous Marvel: The highest peak in the solar system isn't on a planet but on the asteroid Vesta. Rheasilvia central peak towers an impressive 14 miles high. By comparison, Mount Everest is 5.5 miles high.

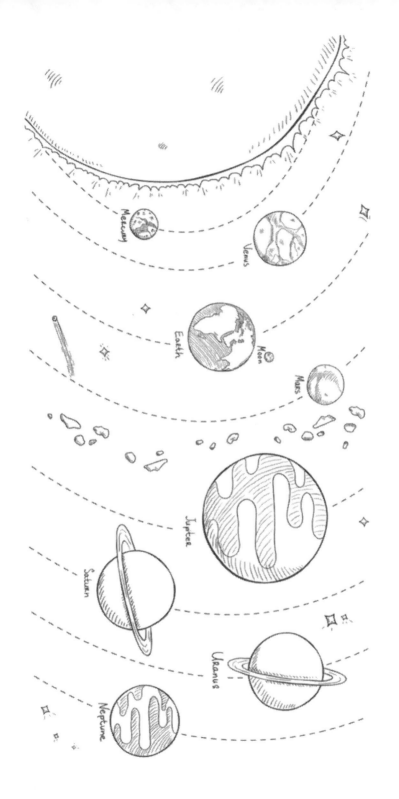

How did this start?

Mainstream Idea

Embark on a journey through time and space, to the very genesis of our solar system, a cosmic tale that begins about 4.6 billion years ago in a cloud of gas and dust, swirling in the vastness of space. This is the story of the birth of our Sun and its planetary family, a narrative woven from the threads of astronomy, geology, and the ever-evolving understanding of the cosmos.

Our solar system's story begins in a giant molecular cloud, known as a nebula. These nebulae are the cradles of star formation, vast and cold, composed mainly of hydrogen and helium, with traces of other elements. Within this particular nebula, something remarkable happened. Perhaps triggered by the shockwave of a nearby supernova, a part of this cloud began to collapse under its own gravity. As it collapsed, it spun, forming a rotating disk of gas and dust - the protoplanetary disk.

At the heart of this collapsing cloud, where the pressure and temperature rose exponentially, the core ignited, giving birth to a new star - our Sun. This process, known as nuclear fusion, transformed hydrogen into helium, releasing enormous amounts of energy, lighting up the young solar system. The Sun, like a benevolent monarch, would come to dominate the solar system, holding its planets in a gravitational embrace.

Around the young Sun, the remaining cloud of gas and dust didn't remain idle. In this protoplanetary disk, particles of dust and ice started to collide and stick together, gradually growing into larger bodies - the building blocks of planets, known as planetesimals. Over millions of years, these planetesimals accreted more and more material, growing into the planets we know today.

Closest to the Sun, where it was too hot for ice to survive, the planetesimals formed from rock and metal, giving rise to the terrestrial planets: Mercury, Venus, Earth, and Mars. These rocky worlds, each with its unique story, would go on to carve their own paths in the solar system. Earth, our home, found itself in the 'Goldilocks zone', where conditions were just right for life to emerge and flourish.

Further from the Sun, where it was colder, ice could survive. Here, planetesimals grew larger, accreting not only rock and metal but also ice. This allowed them to grow massive enough to·capture hydrogen and helium from the nebula, forming the gas giants: Jupiter and Saturn. Beyond them, the ice giants Uranus and Neptune formed, composed mainly of water, ammonia, and methane ices.

The planets were not alone in their dance around the Sun. They were accompanied by moons, each with its own origin story. Some moons formed alongside their planets, while others were captured from the surrounding space. Between Mars and Jupiter lies the asteroid belt, a collection of rocky remnants from the solar system's formation, a testament to the dynamic and sometimes chaotic process of planet formation.

Beyond Neptune lies the Kuiper Belt, a region filled with icy bodies, where Pluto and other dwarf planets reside. This distant region is like a time capsule, preserving the conditions of the early solar system.

Throughout this grand cosmic dance, the Sun has remained the anchor of the solar system, its gravitational pull keeping the planets in their orbits. It has transformed over billions of years and will continue to do so, eventually swelling into a red giant before settling down as a white dwarf.

This narrative of our solar system's formation is the result of centuries of astronomical observations, space missions, and scientific inquiry. It's a story that's continuously being updated and refined as new discoveries are made. From the rocky inner planets to the gas and ice giants, from the moons to the distant Kuiper Belt, our solar system is a dynamic, ever-evolving place, each part of it a piece of the puzzle in understanding our cosmic origins.

Velikovsky

Immanuel Velikovsky (1895-1979) was a controversial figure known for his unconventional theories about the history of the solar system. His most famous work, "Worlds in Collision" (1950), postulated that many of the Earth's geological features and historical events could be explained by the close approach of other planets in the solar system, specifically Venus and Mars. Velikovsky's vision is a spellbinding fusion of astronomy, history, and mythology, presenting a universe where celestial mechanics and ancient narratives intertwine.

Velikovsky's captivating narrative weaves a tale of celestial drama, beginning with Venus. He imagines it as a fiery comet, birthed tumultuously from Jupiter. He draws parallels to Greek mythology, equating the goddess Athena with Venus. Athena's dramatic emergence from Zeus (Jupiter) symbolizes, in his view, Venus's ejection from Jupiter. In his hypothesis, this astral rebel once made a perilous journey near Earth, setting off catastrophic events reminiscent of the biblical plagues of Egypt.

Picture rivers turning to blood, endless days of darkness, and fire raining from the sky. Velikovsky interprets these not as mere allegories but as historical accounts of Venus's chaotic flyby. He posits that the biblical plague of darkness was caused by a massive dust cloud from Venus enveloping Earth, and the fire falling from the sky was ignited by hydrocarbons in Venus's tail reacting with Earth's atmosphere.

In Velikovsky's narrative, Mars plays a pivotal role in the celestial drama following Venus's turbulent path. He theorizes that the gravitational upheaval caused by Venus's close encounters with Earth had a destabilizing effect on Mars's orbit. This led to a series of close approaches of Mars to Earth, each with significant consequences. These Martian near-misses were not mere flybys but dramatic events that left a tangible mark on Earth and its history. He speculates that Mars, during these encounters, would have appeared as a fiery, menacing body in the sky, much larger than any celestial object known to humans at that time.

The gravitational effects of these encounters, he suggests, could have caused significant geological and climatic upheavals on Earth – triggering volcanic eruptions, earthquakes, and even altering the planet's axis and rotation. He points to stories across different cultures that describe a time when Mars took on a fearsome aspect in the sky, leading to widespread destruction on Earth. These narratives, he proposes, are not myth but historical accounts of

Mars's close approaches. For example, he interprets the Norse myths of Ragnarok, which describe a series of natural disasters and the subsequent flooding of the world, as a potential record of Mars's catastrophic impact on Earth.

He suggests that Mars was revered and feared as a god of war not because of its reddish appearance alone, but due to the actual historical events that people associated with this planet – events that were catastrophic enough to be etched in the collective memory of various civilizations and passed down through generations in the form of myths and religious beliefs.

In Velikovsky's interpretation of Joshua's Long Day as a global event, he examines the biblical account of the sun standing still during the Battle of Gibeon. He views this as evidence of a significant disturbance in Earth's rotation, potentially caused by Venus' close approach. Velikovsky strengthens his hypothesis with parallel accounts from various cultures, suggesting a universally witnessed phenomenon. These include:

- The Ojibwe (Native American) Legend: A tale describes a prolonged period of darkness, which Velikovsky correlates with the biblical account of an extended day, suggesting a disruption in Earth's rotational period.
- Ancient Chinese Records: Chronicles from this period in China mention a 'long day', a phenomenon that aligns with Velikovsky's hypothesis of a global event affecting Earth's rotation.
- Hindu Scriptures: In Indian texts, there are references to the sun delaying its setting, particularly in the context of epic battles in texts like the Mahabharata, which Velikovsky interprets as another cultural memory of the same event.

Velikovsky makes the argument that memories across the globe shared for generations had to come from some shared seed. Though his theories have been shunned by modern science, they spark curiosity. Perhaps an aspiring scientist will be inspired to prove or disprove Velikovsky when our tools develop further and will stumble into the right idea. Inspiration comes from everywhere.

Outrageous Ideas

The Elusive "Planet Nine": Imagine a hidden giant, lurking in the shadows of our solar system. This is the "Planet Nine" hypothesis, brought to us in 2016 by astronomers Konstantin Batygin and Mike Brown from the California Institute of Technology. They suggest a massive, unseen planet, far beyond Neptune, orchestrating the strange ballet of orbits in the Kuiper Belt. Despite the valiant efforts of astronomers, this enigmatic planet remains a wraith in our cosmic neighborhood, unseen but perhaps not unfound, fueling debates and dreams of what might lie in the uncharted fringes of our solar system.

Mars' Methane Enigma: Mars, with its desolate beauty, hides a tantalizing secret – the curious case of fluctuating methane levels. The Mars Curiosity rover, a robotic detective on the Red Planet, has sniffed out this gas, commonly produced by life on Earth. This discovery, echoed by other missions like ESA's Mars Express, whispers the thrilling possibility of life, yet the inconsistency in findings veils the truth in mystery. What is the source of Mars' methane? The question hangs in the Martian air, challenging and intriguing scientists.

The Age of Saturn's Rings – A Celestial Debate: Saturn, adorned with its majestic rings, is at the center of an astronomical debate. Are these glittering rings a relatively recent addition, born from the cosmic destruction of a moon a mere 100 million years ago? Or are they as ancient as the solar system itself, 4.5 billion years old, witnesses to the sun's birth and the planetary dance that followed? This debate is more than academic; it's a quest to understand the very history and evolution of our solar neighborhood.

The Mystery of 'Oumuamua: In 2017, an interstellar voyager named 'Oumuamua sailed through our solar system, its peculiar shape and trajectory igniting imaginations and controversies. Was this object, first thought to be a comet, actually a messenger from another world, an alien artifact? While the consensus leans toward 'Oumuamua being a natural interstellar object, its true nature remains unknown.

Lunar Water Mysteries: Our Moon, long thought to be a barren, dry world, has revealed its secret reserves of water. Discoveries of water ice in the lunar polar regions have overturned old beliefs, but questions abound. The origins, quantities, and distribution of this lunar water are subjects of fervent research and debate. This revelation is not just a scientific curiosity; it holds the key to future lunar exploration and perhaps even the secrets of life's origins.

Moon

Fun Facts

Celestial Illusion: The Sun and Moon appear the same size from Earth due to a cosmic coincidence: the Sun is 400 times larger but also 400 times farther away, creating a perfect visual balance in our sky.

Earth's Loyal Companion: Our Moon, an enchanting celestial body, is the fifth-largest moon in the solar system and Earth's only natural satellite. Its steady orbit and phases have captivated human imagination for millennia.

Moon's Unique Geometry: The Moon has a subtly egg-shaped form, with its larger end affectionately nodding towards Earth. This distinctive shape results from Earth's gravitational pull, a cosmic dance of celestial mechanics.

The Moon's Wispy Atmosphere: Unlike Earth's robust atmosphere, the Moon's exosphere is a delicate veil of gases, including hydrogen, helium, and neon. This thin layer offers no refuge from the harshness of space, leaving the lunar surface vulnerable to meteor impacts and solar radiation.

A World of Extremes: The Moon's surface is a dramatic landscape of stark contrasts, featuring towering mountains, deep canyons, and ancient craters. Among these, Valles Schröteri stands out as a grand canyon over 180 miles (300 kilometers) long, a silent witness to the Moon's geological history.

Helium-3, Lunar Treasure: The Moon is rich in helium-3, a rare isotope with potential as a clean energy source for nuclear fusion. This makes the Moon an intriguing focus for future energy solutions.

Temperature Rollercoaster: The Moon experiences one of the most extreme temperature variations in the solar system. Its surface heats up to a blistering 260°F (127°C) during the lunar day and plunges to a frigid -280°F (-173°C) at night, reflecting its lack of atmosphere. The Moon's South Pole is among the coldest places in the solar system, with temperatures dropping to an unimaginable -249°C (-416°F).

Shaking Lunar Ground: Moonquakes, akin to earthquakes, occur due to the gravitational tug-of-war with Earth. These quakes provide valuable insights into the Moon's interior structure and its dynamic relationship with our planet.

Master of Tides: The Moon's gravitational influence is the primary force driving the rhythmic rise and fall of Earth's ocean tides, showcasing a profound natural synergy between the two celestial bodies.

A Historic Leap for Mankind: The Moon holds a unique place in human history as the first extraterrestrial body to be visited by humans. The Apollo 11 mission in 1969 marked a milestone in space exploration and human achievement.

Comparative Dimensions: The Moon's diameter is about a quarter of Earth's, approximately the width of the United States. This size comparison offers a tangible sense of the Moon's presence in our night sky.

Two Faces of the Moon: The Moon's near side is permanently Earth-facing due to synchronous rotation, while the far side, often mislabeled as 'dark,' receives just as much sunlight and remains largely unexplored.

A Darker Reality: Contrary to its bright appearance in our night sky, the Moon's surface is dark, akin to coal. It's composed of basaltic rocks, which reflect sunlight, making it a beacon in the night.

Echoes of a Magnetic Past: The presence of magnetized rocks on the Moon suggests it once had a magnetic field. These remnants offer clues to understanding the Moon's early history and its once-active core.

Moon's Gradual Goodbye: The Moon is slowly drifting away from Earth at a rate of 1.5 inch (3.8 cm) per year. This gradual separation is a result of complex gravitational interactions and has long-term implications for both celestial bodies.

The Great Lunar Basin: The Moon's largest impact crater, the South Pole-Aitken Basin, is a colossal depression. Over 1,500 miles (2,500 kilometers) in diameter and 8 miles (13 kilometers) deep, it's one of the most striking features in the solar system.

Brightest After the Sun: The Moon, the second brightest object in our night sky, serves as a nocturnal sun, guiding and inspiring humanity throughout history.

More Than Meets the Eye: Due to lunar libration, we can see about 59% of the Moon's surface over time, slightly more than the half constantly facing us, offering a slightly shifting lunar vista.

Eccentric Orbit: The Moon's path around Earth is an ellipse, not a perfect circle. This elliptical orbit causes the varying sizes of the Moon as seen from Earth, adding to its mystique in our skies.

A Cosmic Collision's Child: The Moon is believed to have formed from debris after a Mars-sized body collided with Earth about 4.5 billion years ago. This tumultuous origin story adds to the Moon's mystique and significance in understanding planetary formation.

Lunar Size Illusions: The Moon's orbit creates the illusion of changing size. When closest to Earth, it appears as a larger 'supermoon,' and when farther, it shrinks to a 'micromoon,' adding to its celestial allure.

Flags on the Lunar Surface: The Moon hosts five U.S. flags, left by Apollo astronauts. These symbols of human exploration, now likely bleached white by solar radiation, are silent witnesses to our journey into space.

Lunar vs. Terrestrial Real Estate: The Moon's surface area is less than that of Asia, providing a perspective on its size compared to Earth and highlighting the vastness of our home planet.

Feather-Light Gravity: The Moon's gravity is just one-sixth of Earth's, meaning objects and astronauts feel much lighter there. This reduced gravity has been a source of both challenge and amusement for lunar explorers.

Regolith Riches: The Moon's surface is covered in regolith, a fine lunar soil peppered with tiny glass beads formed by meteor impacts. This unique lunar soil holds secrets to the Moon's past and potential resources for future exploration.

A Moonstruck Melody: The Moon became the venue for a unique musical moment when astronaut Alan Shepard played "Fly Me to the Moon" during the Apollo 14 mission, adding a whimsical note to lunar exploration.

Scent of the Moon: According to Apollo astronauts, the Moon's soil has a distinctive smell akin to spent gunpowder. This surprising sensory detail adds to the mysteries of the lunar surface.

Shadows of Eclipses: The Moon casts two types of shadows - the penumbra and the umbra. These shadows play a crucial role in creating the mesmerizing phenomena of partial and total solar eclipses, captivating observers on Earth.

The Moon's Shrinking Secrets: Our Moon is gradually shrinking over time, causing it to wrinkle like a raisin! This surprising phenomenon, due to its cooling interior, has resulted in the formation of "moonquakes" that reshape its surface. Even our celestial neighbor has its own set of growing pains!

Timeless Lunar Footprints: The footprints left by Apollo astronauts on the moon are destined for eons of fame, remaining undisturbed for millions of years in the lunar silence since there is no wind or water to erode them.

Water Mysteries - Moon's Icy Secrets: The discovery of water ice on the Moon opens a chapter filled with questions and possibilities. How did this life-sustaining substance arrive on the Moon? Was it a gift from comets, or did it emerge from the Moon's own hidden depths? This water, a source of intrigue and potential, paints the Moon not as a barren wasteland but as a keeper of life's essential ingredient.

The Moon's Interior - A Tectonic Puzzle: Is the Moon tectonically active? The debate over this question, spurred by data from ancient seismometers, adds depth to our understanding of the Moon's internal workings. Whether the Moon's quakes are echoes of its cooling heart or the scars of meteorite impacts, they remind us that the Moon is a dynamic world, with secrets still to unveil.

How did the Moon Happen?

In the grand cosmic ballet, the origin of Earth's Moon is a story that captures the imagination, a tale woven from the very fabric of the solar system. This celestial narrative, as understood by mainstream science, is not only about the birth of a moon but also about a dramatic and violent event in the early history of our planet.

Our story begins over 4.5 billion years ago, in the nascent days of the solar system. The Earth was young, a protoplanet in the process of formation, amidst a swirling dance of cosmic debris. The environment was chaotic, a time marked by frequent collisions and the constant reshaping of celestial bodies.

At the heart of the Moon's origin story is the Giant Impact Hypothesis, the prevailing scientific theory that describes a cataclysmic event shaping the destiny of both Earth and its satellite. According to this hypothesis, a Mars-sized protoplanet, often named Theia, collided with the young Earth in a titanic clash. This impact was not a mere brush or a graze but a colossal collision that would redefine the structure of Earth and give birth to the Moon.

The impact of Theia was so immense that it literally shook Earth to its core. The energy released melted large portions of Earth and completely disintegrated Theia. From this fiery cataclysm, a vast cloud of debris was ejected into orbit around Earth. This debris, a mixture of material from both Earth and Theia, began its own journey of transformation.

In the orbit around the reeling Earth, the ejected debris started to coalesce. Gravity, the eternal sculptor, worked its magic, pulling the fragments together. Over time, these fragments of rock and metal began to clump and merge, gradually forming larger bodies. Through the process of accretion, these pieces eventually gathered to form a single, larger celestial body – the Moon.

The newly formed Moon was much closer to Earth than it is now, and its gravitational influence was profound. It played a crucial role in stabilizing Earth's tilt and rotation, a factor that would become critical for the development of a stable climate and the evolution of life. The gravitational interaction between Earth and the Moon also led to tidal forces, which played a significant role in shaping the geological and biological development of our planet.

As the Moon cooled, its surface began to solidify. The early Moon experienced intense bombardment from meteorites and comets, a common occurrence in the young solar system. This bombardment led to the formation of the Moon's craters and its maria, the large, dark basaltic plains that are visible from Earth.

The story of the Moon's formation is far from complete. Each lunar mission, each sample returned, and each observation adds a new chapter to this ongoing narrative. From the Apollo missions to the latest lunar probes, the Moon continues to reveal its secrets, giving rise to even more theories of not only its own history but also the history of Earth and the solar system.

That's the most widely accepted hypothesis for the origin of the moon, but it's by no means perfect. There is no way yet to confirm a giant impact created the moon, and our sense of how the magma ocean cooled down into the dry, gray rock we see now is still very hazy. About 10 years ago, we discovered evidence of water on the moon—something that's a bit difficult to reconcile with an impact hypothesis. Getting to the bottom of the moon's past requires the sort of on-the-ground work we've done to unravel Earth's own history.

Outrageous Ideas

In the realm of celestial mysteries, few are as enchanting and thought-provoking as the origin of Earth's Moon.

Capture Theory: This theory posits that the Moon was formed elsewhere and captured by Earth's gravity. Despite its imaginative appeal, this theory is challenged by the low likelihood of such an event and doesn't explain the isotopic similarities between Earth and the Moon.

Fission Theory: Suggested by George Darwin, son of Charles Darwin, this theory proposes that the Moon was once part of Earth and separated, possibly where the Pacific Ocean now lies. Current understandings of physics make this theory unlikely. Most scientists discount the fission hypothesis, saying that Earth could not have been spinning fast enough to expel a huge blob of rock.

One 2010 study suggested that a natural nuclear explosion, set up by the superconcentration of radioactive elements, may have provided the kick to dislodge a moon-size piece of the early Earth into orbit. However, the Moon's age presents a problem for most proponents of the fission theory. Based on the analysis of Moon rocks brought back by the Apollo missions, some researchers have suggested that the Moon is around 4.5 billion years old, contemporary to the formation of Earth. This might contradict the widely accepted theory that the Moon was formed from the debris left over after a collision between Earth and a Mars-sized body known as Theia, which is thought to have occurred around 4.5 billion years ago, unless the moon formed in hours rather than millions of years. If the Moon rocks were this old, they would have had to solidify soon after the impact by Theia, which some scientists argue is unlikely or if the fission theory holds, the Moon would have had to fissure from the Earth as the Earth was forming.

Hollow Moon Theory: This hypothesis suggests the Moon might be hollow, based on interpretations of seismic activities from the Apollo missions. However, scientific consensus, informed by seismic data, points to a Moon with a thin crust, extensive mantle, and dense core. NASA and many scientists say the Moon has an Earth-like core. But the moon has a mass of only 1.2% of the Earth while being 1/4 the diameter of the Earth. So that is not comparable. Perhaps our Moon is just very light for its size.

Spaceship Moon Theory: This intriguing theory suggests the Moon might be an artificial structure, created by advanced beings. Proponents point to several lunar anomalies to support:

- Strange Seismic Activity: Moonquakes recorded by Apollo mission seismometers led to descriptions of the Moon ringing "like a bell," speculated to indicate hollowness or artificiality. Scientific explanations, however, suggest a more rigid surface compared to Earth due to a lack of water, causing vibrations to travel more cleanly.
- Unusual Crater Depth: Observations that lunar craters have uniform depths despite varying impact scales have led to speculation about a harder shell beneath the surface, though this is scientifically explained by isostatic equilibrium, the idea that the lighter crust must be floating on the denser underlying mantle much the way an iceberg bobs in the water. In effect the Moon's mantle pushes up against the crater formations to equalize them.
- Moon's Composition and Brightness: The Moon's high reflectiveness is seen by some as indicative of an artificial surface. However, the Moon's albedo (reflectiveness) is just 0.12, meaning it reflects only 12% of sunlight, and its brightness is due to proximity to Earth.
- Perfect Orbit and Size: The precise nature of lunar eclipses has been seen as too perfect to be natural, though this is generally attributed to natural celestial mechanics.
- Moon Rock Composition: During the Apollo missions, astronauts brought back Moon rocks. Some proponents claim these rocks contain processed metals like brass, mica, and the elements Uranium 236 and Neptunium 237, which are not naturally occurring. Uranium 236 and Neptunium 237 are byproducts of nuclear reactions. The scientific consensus is that these findings would be highly unusual and contrary to accepted lunar geology.

- Cave Paintings: Cave paintings dating to 40k years ago show many constellations that we would recognize today, but they fail to show our moon. Art from 14,000 years ago starts to incorporate our moon.

There is significant debate about what has been found in Moon rocks as they are not available for wide study. There may yet be an even more wild story behind the creation of our Moon.

Oceans

Fun Facts

The Atlantic Ocean's Growing Spree: The Atlantic Ocean is slowly but steadily expanding, stretching itself by about 1 inch (2.5 cm) each year. This growth is driven by the movement of tectonic plates, which are constantly reshaping our planet's surface.

The Shrinking Pacific: In a grand geologic dance, as the Atlantic grows, the Pacific Ocean is gently contracting by about .4 inch (1 cm) per year. This subtle shift is a reminder of the ever-changing nature of Earth's surface, molded by the same tectonic forces.

Gold-Infused Waters: The ocean's waters hold a whisper of gold in every liter, amounting to 13 billionths of a gram. Collectively, this dissolved gold could theoretically provide each person on Earth with about 9 pounds of this precious metal, creating a liquid treasure trove.

Salty Secrets Revealed: The ocean's salinity isn't just from the land but also from underwater volcanoes. These natural wonders contribute minerals and salts from the Earth's interior, seasoning the sea with flavors from deep within our planet.

Hidden Underwater Worlds: The ocean's depths are home to mysterious brine pools and underwater rivers and lakes. These surreal formations, denser and saltier than the surrounding seawater, create unique ecosystems resembling oases in an underwater desert.

The Elusive Depths: The Mariana Trench, Earth's deepest point, remains more mysterious than the moon. Fewer people have visited this enigmatic abyss, making it a testament to the challenges and allure of deep-sea exploration.

Blue Whale: The Ocean's Leviathan: The blue whale, larger than even the mightiest dinosaurs, holds the title of the largest animal ever known to exist. These gentle giants, measuring up to 100 feet in length, glide through the oceans with a grace that belies their size.

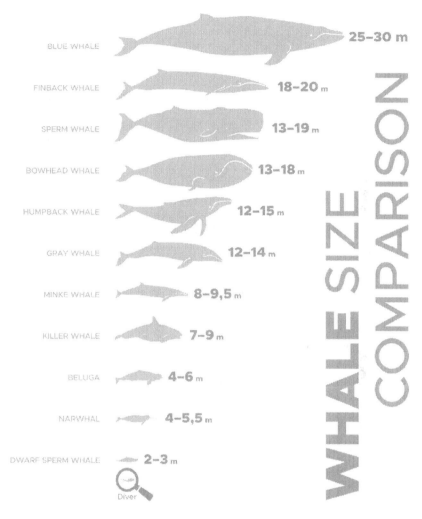

WHALE SIZE COMPARISON

BLUE WHALE	25–30 m
FINBACK WHALE	18–20 m
SPERM WHALE	13–19 m
BOWHEAD WHALE	13–18 m
HUMPBACK WHALE	12–15 m
GRAY WHALE	12–14 m
MINKE WHALE	8–9,5 m
KILLER WHALE	7–9 m
BELUGA	4–6 m
NARWHAL	4–5,5 m
DWARF SPERM WHALE	2–3 m

Diver

Zombie Worms' Banquet: The deep seabed is a dining hall for bone-eating worms. These 'zombie worms' feast on the skeletons of whales and other marine giants, thriving in a world where sunlight never reaches.

A Living Giant: The Great Barrier Reef, an underwater spectacle visible from space, is not just a coral reef but the largest living structure on Earth. Stretching over 1,400 miles (2,300 kilometers) long, covering over 133,000 square miles (almost 350,000 square km), it's a bustling underwater city teeming with diverse marine life.

Ocean, The Life-Rich Realm: Covering 71% of Earth's surface, the ocean is a buzzing hub of biodiversity. It's estimated to house between 50-80% of all life on our planet, a testament to its role as a cradle of life.

Volcanic Undersea World: Beneath the ocean's surface, a hidden world of volcanic activity thrives. An estimated 80% of Earth's volcanic eruptions occur underwater, creating a landscape of fire and water in the depths.

The Ocean's Climate Role: The ocean is a crucial player in our planet's climate, absorbing about 30% of human-made carbon dioxide. This significant role helps mitigate the impact of climate change, highlighting the ocean's importance in our global ecosystem.

Underwater Mountain Majesty: The Mid-Atlantic Ridge is a mountain range like no other, stretching beneath the ocean's surface. At over five times longer than the Andes, it's a colossal feature of our planet's geology, mostly hidden from view.

Majestic Underwater Waterfalls: The Denmark Strait houses an underwater waterfall far grander than any on land. Here, a massive flow of cold water plunges into the ocean depths, an invisible yet mighty force shaping the marine environment.

Mysterious Black Smokers: Deep on the ocean floor, 'black smokers' form otherworldly structures. These hydrothermal vents spew superheated, mineral-rich water, creating unique habitats teeming with specialized life forms.

Crushing Depths: The pressure at the Mariana Trench's deepest point is like bearing the weight of 50 jumbo jets stacked on top of you. It's a testament to the extreme conditions that exist in the deepest parts of our oceans.

The Ocean's Layered Cake: The ocean is divided into five distinct layers: sunlight, twilight, midnight, abyss, and trench, each with its unique ecosystem. From the sunlit surface waters to the mysterious deep sea, each layer offers a different glimpse into the complexity of marine life.

Ocean Zones

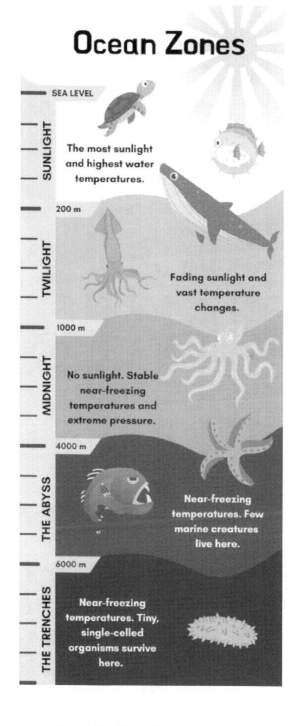

SEA LEVEL

SUNLIGHT

The most sunlight and highest water temperatures.

200 m

TWILIGHT

Fading sunlight and vast temperature changes.

1000 m

MIDNIGHT

No sunlight. Stable near-freezing temperatures and extreme pressure.

4000 m

THE ABYSS

Near-freezing temperatures. Few marine creatures live here.

6000 m

THE TRENCHES

Near-freezing temperatures. Tiny, single-celled organisms survive here.

A Treasure Trove Below: The ocean bed holds a wealth of historical artifacts with over 3 million shipwrecks lying in its depths, more than all the world's museums combined. From sunken cities to ancient relics, the sea guards countless secrets of human history.

Mineral-Rich Seas: The oceans are rich in critical minerals, with 37 out of 50 essential types found in their depths. This vast mineral kingdom beneath the waves is an untapped resource with the potential to shape our future.

The Ocean's Climatic Pulse: The ocean acts as Earth's 'heart,' regulating and influencing our climate. This massive, flowing system is vital to maintaining the balance of our planet's health.

The Ocean's White Noise Symphony: The ocean is filled with a constant, low-frequency hum, the sound of countless marine creatures moving and communicating. This underwater symphony is an ever-present backdrop to the ocean's bustling life.

The Uncharted Waters: Despite its vastness, less than 10% of the world's oceans have been thoroughly explored and mapped. This leaves a vast majority of this aquatic world shrouded in mystery, waiting to be discovered.

The Drifting Seafloor: The ocean floor is in constant motion, reshaping the foundation of our oceans. This slow, relentless movement is a reminder of the dynamic nature of our planet.

Ocean's Lunar Comparison: The Pacific Ocean's expanse is so vast that it exceeds the width of the moon. This comparison offers a cosmic perspective on the sheer scale of our own blue planet.

Priorities: Ocean exploration spending approached $1.4 billion in 2022 with $317 million for the Ocean Exploration and Research program, $268 million for Ocean and Coastal Mapping, and $813 million for hydrographic surveying. In contrast, NASA's funding for space exploration in 2022 was $24 billion which is the bulk of space exploration spending but does not include the Army, Navy, Air Force and other agency space exploration spending.

Hidden Ocean: A huge supply of water is hidden 400 miles underground stored in rock known as "ringwoodite." It's not sloshing around or ready for surfing, but it appears to be 3-times as much water as we have on the surface!

Unsolved Mysteries

It Glows!: It's wrong to say there's no light in the depths of the ocean. There's light, it just doesn't come from the sun. Deep in the ocean (and also on the surface), divers find other-worldly displays of bioluminescence, sparkling like fireworks in the dark. Huge numbers of deep-water creatures light up in some way. Dive into the depths of the ocean, and you're greeted with a mystical light show, courtesy of its inhabitants.

This phenomenon of bioluminescence, a natural form of light emission, is a fascinating adaptation seen in many marine creatures. It's a world where creatures like jellyfish, squids, and even some fish light up the underwater darkness. The bioluminescence serves various purposes – as a defense mechanism to startle predators, a way to attract mates, or even as a cunning strategy to lure unsuspecting prey. This glowing spectacle isn't just a stunning display; it's a vital part of life in the ocean's depths, a brilliant survival strategy in the vast and mysterious marine world.

Beached: The phenomenon of whales beaching themselves is both heart-wrenching and puzzling. Each year, these majestic creatures end up stranded on beaches, a sight that often leaves scientists and conservationists scrambling for answers. The causes behind these strandings are complex and multifaceted. While human impact on the oceans, such as noise pollution and habitat changes, may be a contributor, the exact reasons vary. From solar and magnetic activities that could disorient whales, to the effects of increasing ocean traffic, these strandings appear to be increasing. Understanding why these strandings occur is not just a scientific pursuit; it's crucial for the conservation of these magnificent ocean giants.

Hiding Among Us: The ocean itself is one of the world's biggest mysteries. The National Ocean Service states that more than 80 percent of our planet's oceans are still unmapped, unobserved, and unexplored, which makes up about 139 million square miles of potential revelations. By point of comparison, all of the land on Earth totals 57million square miles. In the vast and largely uncharted world of our oceans, surprises abound, as evidenced by the discovery of a pink manta ray. T

his unique creature, captured in the waters off Lady Elliot Island in Australia's Great Barrier Reef by photographer Kristian Laine, stands out with its unusual pink belly. Initially thought to be a camera glitch, this manta ray, affectionately nicknamed Inspector Clouseau, is a biological wonder. Identified in 2015 and seen fewer than a dozen times, Clouseau's distinct pink hue is attributed to a rare genetic mutation. This discovery challenges our understanding of manta rays, generally known for their black and white appearance, essential for camouflage and hunting. Clouseau's survival and coloration add a colorful chapter to the myriad mysteries hidden in the ocean's depths.

The Milky Sea Phenomenon: A rare and awe-inspiring occurrence transforms vast areas of the ocean surface into a glowing, milky blue expanse at night. Spanning up to 10,000 square miles (16,000 square kilometers), this natural spectacle is believed to be caused by bioluminescent bacteria. Although the precise biological or chemical triggers for such large-scale bioluminescence remain a mystery, these events are often observed in specific areas like the Indian Ocean and near Indonesia. Understanding this phenomenon could unlock secrets about marine ecosystems and the intricate interactions between organisms in our oceans.

The Existence of Sea Monsters (Cryptids): For centuries, sailors have reported encounters with large, unknown creatures in the deep ocean, from sea serpents to giant squids. While many of these tales are likely embellished or based on misidentifications, some have a basis in reality. For instance, the giant squid was considered a myth until carcasses began washing ashore and a live specimen was finally filmed in 2004. Other creatures, like the Loch Ness Monster, continue to elicit debate despite a lack of solid evidence. While it is unlikely that large unknown species remain undiscovered in well-traveled areas like Loch Ness, the vast, unexplored depths of the ocean hold the potential for undiscovered species.

Outrageous Ideas

The Bermuda Triangle: Spanning between Miami, Bermuda, and Puerto Rico, this area has been the subject of numerous tales involving the disappearance of ships and aircraft. While popular culture is rife with theories involving magnetic anomalies, methane hydrates, and even extraterrestrial activities, scientific investigations offer more grounded explanations. Notably, the region is not recognized as unusual by official bodies like the U.S. Board on Geographic Names and NOAA. Research suggests that the number of incidents in the Bermuda Triangle is neither extraordinary nor mysterious, challenging the mystique that surrounds this iconic part of the ocean. Perhaps it's just a matter of stories close to us getting more play time.

The Bimini Road (Underwater Rock Formation): Discovered in the 1960s near the Bimini islands in the Bahamas, this underwater rock formation consists of limestone blocks lined up in what appears to be a road-like structure. Some speculate that this could be the remnants of the lost city of Atlantis. Geological studies suggest that the Bimini Road is a natural geological formation known as beach rock that breaks along joints and can create straight edges, giving the appearance of a man-made structure. However, the debate continues among some researchers and enthusiasts as the formations are not isolated to Bimini. A similar underwater formation though in a ziggurat-like formation rests off the coast of Yonaguni, Japan. Ancient submerged city? Or naturally created?

Crabs' Medical Contribution: The blood of horseshoe crabs plays a crucial role in modern medicine. It is used to detect harmful gram-negative bacteria like Escherichia coli (E. coli) in various medical products, including injectable drugs such as insulin, implantable medical devices like knee replacements, and hospital instruments such as scalpels and IVs. The unique property of horseshoe crab blood is its sensitivity to bacteria, which triggers a clotting reaction around these invaders, protecting the crab's body from toxins. This blood contains a substance called Limulus Amebocyte Lysate (LAL), the only known natural source of a clotting agent used to detect dangerous endotoxins in human medical products. And it's bright blue!

Venomous Ocean Dweller: The blue-ringed octopus, one of the ocean's most toxic creatures, carries venom that is 1,000 times more potent than cyanide. This venom contains a complex mix of substances including tetrodotoxin, histamine, tryptamine, octopamine, taurine, acetylcholine, and dopamine. Bites from a blue-ringed octopus can result in nausea, respiratory arrest, heart failure, severe paralysis, and even death within minutes. There is no antivenom available for this octopus's venom. While the venom has short-lived effects, usually lasting only a few hours, immediate medical attention is critical for survival. Fortunately, bites are rare, with only a few incidents reported annually in Australia, and a limited number of documented deaths globally.

Geology

Fun Facts

The Ice Age Enigma: Ice age terminations are a complex puzzle. While Earth's orbital changes, known as Milankovitch cycles, are thought to trigger these ends, the exact roles of CO_2 and other feedback mechanisms remain a topic of fascinating ongoing research.

Obliquity (axial tilt): The Earth's axis is tilted at an angle as it travels around the Sun. Within 41,000 years (one obliquity cycle) this tilt angle changes and directly influences how extreme our seasons are. The tilt angle changes how much incoming solar radiation arrives in polar regions.

Eccentricity (orbit shape): The shape of the Earth's orbit changes from almost circular to slightly elliptic over approximately 100,000 years. This changes Earth's distance from the sun. The closer the Earth is to the sun, the more solar radiation reaches Earth.

Snowball Earth's Chilly Secret: Imagine our planet, during the Cryogenian period, almost entirely encased in ice, from pole to pole! This 'Snowball Earth' scenario, suggested by geological evidence like tropical glacial deposits, might have sparked the evolution of complex life forms.

Majestic Ice Age Creatures: The Pleistocene epoch was not just a time of ice; it was a realm of giants. Towering ground sloths and fearsome saber-toothed tigers shared the landscape with early humans, adding a dash of wild wonder to the ice age story.

The Vast Reach of Ice Sheets: During the last ice age, colossal ice sheets up to 2 miles thick blanketed large swaths of the Northern Hemisphere. Their weight reshaped Earth's crust, and their melting sculpted landscapes like the Great Lakes and the Midwest's rolling hills.

Climate Lessons from the Past: Ice ages are more than historical footnotes; they're keys to our climatic future. Studying ice cores reveals past greenhouse gas levels, helping us understand Earth's natural climate rhythms and informing predictions about ongoing human and non-human-induced changes.

Sea Level's Dramatic Dance: The last ice age trapped immense water amounts in ice sheets, lowering sea levels by up to 400 feet (120 meters). This exposed land bridges, such as the Bering Land Bridge, enabling human and animal migrations across continents. The subsequent melting reshaped coastlines and affected species distribution.

Pollen's Prehistoric Journey: Trapped in sediment and ice, pollen grains are tiny time capsules. They reveal which plants thrived during different ice age periods, shedding light on climate shifts and ecosystem responses to glacial conditions.

Ocean Currents' Climate Drama: Ice ages saw significant shifts in ocean currents, altering global climates. Changes in the Gulf Stream, for example, affected warm water transport to the North Atlantic, influencing regional weather patterns and contributing to ice age beginnings and ends.

Subglacial Volcanic Wonders: Ice-covered volcanoes, or subglacial volcanoes, offer a unique spectacle. The interaction between molten lava and overlying ice leads to explosive eruptions, creating flat-topped, steep-sided mountains known as tuyas, a testament to volcanic activity during colder times.

Mammoth Steppe's Grandeur: Picture a vast Ice Age grassland stretching from Spain to Canada, the Mammoth Steppe. This extensive habitat was a bustling hub for woolly mammoths and other large creatures, offering a glimpse into the rich biodiversity of the ice age.

Ice Age Artistry: The Ice Age was not just survival; it was also a time of artistic expression. The Lascaux cave paintings in France, dating back around 17,000 years, depict animals and symbols with sophisticated skill, reflecting the rich cultural life of our ancestors in a frozen world.

Bering Land Bridge Saga: The Bering Land Bridge, a vital migration route during the last ice age, connected Asia and North America. This land bridge facilitated the movement of people and animals, profoundly influencing early human history in the Americas.

Resurrecting Ancient Life: Scientists brought back to life a 32,000-year-old plant from fruits buried in Siberian permafrost. Reviving this Pleistocene-era Silene stenophylla offers incredible insights into the resilience and adaptability of ancient life forms.

Glacial Sculpting of Landscapes: The last ice age's massive glaciers carved out deep basins across North America and Northern Europe. These basins, filled with water when the glaciers retreated, formed many of today's lakes, showcasing the lasting impact of glacial forces on our planet's geography.

Megafaunal Extinction Mysteries: The end of the last ice age, about 11,700 years ago, coincided with a dramatic decline in large animals like woolly mammoths. Theories for this mass extinction range from human overhunting to rapid climate changes, highlighting the complex interactions between humans, animals, and the environment.

Ice Age Human Ingenuity: Ice Age humans displayed remarkable adaptability and innovation. They developed specialized tools, clothing, and shelters to survive the extreme cold, showcasing the resourcefulness and creativity of our ancestors in the face of environmental challenges.

Albedo Effect's Climatic Impact: The albedo effect, where ice and snow reflect sunlight, plays a crucial role in Earth's temperature regulation. During ice ages, increased albedo leads to cooler temperatures, while decreased albedo in warmer periods contributes to global warming, illustrating a vital feedback mechanism in our climate system.

Rapid Warming After Ice Ages: The transition from the last ice age to our current warm period saw significant and rapid climate shifts. Within a few thousand years, global temperatures rose about 5°C, leading to major environmental changes and influencing human civilizations' development.

Greenland's Ice Core Chronicles: Greenland's ice sheet, a climatic archive hundreds of thousands of years old, contains ice layers that record past atmospheric compositions, temperature fluctuations, and even volcanic activities, providing valuable insights into Earth's climatic history.

Antarctica's Forested History: Fossil evidence reveals that parts of Antarctica were once covered in forests during warmer periods between ice ages. These forested landscapes, existing millions of years ago, offer a stark contrast to today's icy terrain and shed light on Earth's climatic past.

Foraminifera's Climate Tales: Tiny marine organisms, foraminifera, are key to reconstructing past climates. During ice ages, as large volumes of water are locked in ice sheets, the remaining seawater becomes enriched in the heavier oxygen isotope. Their shells' oxygen isotope ratios vary with seawater temperature, revealing past ocean temperatures and ice volumes, unlocking secrets of Earth's climatic history.

Mysterious Formations

The Eye of the Sahara: Located in Mauritania's expansive landscape, this striking natural wonder, with its concentric circles spanning 28 miles, captivates the eye and stirs the imagination.

Originally, geologists speculated that an asteroid might have sculpted this vast bullseye, a cosmic fingerprint etched into Earth's surface. However, the lack of melted rock typically associated with such celestial collisions cast doubt on this theory. Similarly, the absence of volcanic residues dismissed the idea of a volcanic birth for this enigmatic structure.

Those intrigued by myth have posited that these mysterious rings could be the remnants of the lost city of Atlantis, a legendary island described by Plato.

The most recent and compelling scientific explanation dives deep into Earth's geological history. The Eye of the Sahara is thought to be an eroded, collapsed geological dome. This fascinating formation possibly dates back to the era of Pangea, the ancient supercontinent. About 100 million years ago, as Pangea was splitting apart, monumental geological forces might have pushed ancient rocks, from as deep as 125 miles beneath the Earth's crust, to the surface. These rocks predate life on Earth, making the Eye not only a geological wonder but also a window into our planet's deep past.

Great Unconformity: This fascinating anomaly is like a missing page in our planet's history book, where layers of rock, spanning nearly a billion years, have simply vanished.

The Great Unconformity is most dramatically showcased in the majestic stratigraphy of the Grand Canyon. Here, a stark contrast is visible between the fossil-rich Cambrian rocks, dating back about 540 million years, and the ancient, barren basement rocks formed around 1 billion years ago. This leaves us pondering, what befell the geological records in between?

Enter the captivating theory of "Snowball Earth." About 700 million years ago, our planet might have been swathed in ice, a frozen world far removed from today's vibrant Earth. During this icy epoch, colossal glaciers, like nature's great erasers, scoured the Earth's surface. These glacial giants, aided by sediments acting as natural lubricants, possibly scraped away vast swaths of the planet's crust.

Imagine these relentless glaciers, grinding and moving, pushing the scraped-off crust into the oceans. Here, in the depths of these ancient waters, the Earth's tectonic forces came into play. The subducting tectonic plates, like giant conveyor belts, pulled this crustal material down into the Earth's mantle, effectively recycling it.

This dramatic process could explain the missing geological chapters. However, a lingering mystery remains – the gap between the end of the Snowball Earth around 635 million years ago and the dawn of the Cambrian period, a gap spanning millions of years.

Fairy Circles: Up close, the fairy circles in the Namib Desert are just circular patches of bare red earth, surrounded by tufts of grass. But from a bird's-eye view, these spots stretch endlessly across the arid landscape, creating a regular polka-dot pattern. Folktales claim the spots are the gods' footprints, but scientists have searched for an evidence-based explanation.

At first, some proposed that the circles are created when plants compete for water: The root systems of the successful vegetation dominate the ground, while smaller plants are unable to compete, leaving bare patches of desert. In 2017, a promising new theory appeared in the journal Nature. Excavations of several circles revealed termite nests under each one, implying the circles were created by the termites eating the vegetation above their territory, allowing desert grasses to flourish only between each nest. Ecologists modeled both the plant-competition and hungry-termite theories and found that both supported conditions conducive to fairy circles.

Nastapoka Arc: In the southeast corner of Hudson Bay, Canada, lies a near-perfect arc. The mysterious half-circle, also known as the Hudson Bay Arc, was first thought to be an impact crater from a meteorite. But none of the usual confirming evidence, such as shatter cones or unusual melted rocks, has been found in the vicinity. The most commonly accepted theory for the arc, based on geological evidence collected in the 1970s and later, is that it is a boundary formed when one shelf of rock was pushed under another other. That doesn't explain how or why it is so perfectly round. Such geometric perfection is rare in natural geological formations, which are often shaped by chaotic and complex forces.

Yamal Craters: In 2014, a helicopter pilot flying over the Yamal Peninsula in Siberia, which juts into the Kara Sea, noticed an enormous hole in the permafrost. Scientists rushed to analyze the nearly 100-foot-wide crater to determine its origin. A meteorite impact, a natural gas explosion, or alien interference were all floated as possible causes.

Tests conducted at the bottom of these craters revealed extraordinarily high levels of methane. This clue points to an explosion, a dramatic release of pent-up gases. But what triggered this sudden outburst? Some scientists suggest that a series of unusually warm summers could have played a role, warming the Arctic region and destabilizing the frozen ground. However, there's another twist in this icy tale. Some researchers argue that these craters might not be the result of a sudden, explosive event. Instead, they could represent a more gradual process – the slow, steady collapse of the permafrost itself as nature intended.

The Holocene Epoch dawned about 11,700 years ago following the retreat of the colossal ice sheets of the last Ice Age, marking a period of relative warmth and climate stability – a stark contrast to the icy world that preceded it.

The Holocene is but a chapter in Earth's grand climatic narrative, characterized by its rhythmic dance of warming and cooling cycles. These cycles are driven by the natural ebb and flow of Earth's orbit, tilt, solar radiation, and ocean currents. The Holocene's warmth is not an anomaly but a testament to Earth's cyclical climate rhythm.

Yet, one of the most captivating phenomena in this era is the transformation of the permafrost. Permafrost, a silent giant lying beneath the polar landscapes, encapsulates a frozen history of our planet. In the warmth of the Holocene, this permafrost is undergoing a slow but significant thaw. This thaw reveals a world beneath our feet that has remained locked in time for thousands of years. It's a world brimming with ancient organic material, and as it thaws, it whispers secrets of past ecosystems through the release of greenhouse gases like methane and carbon dioxide.

But the thawing of permafrost is more than just an echo of the past; it's a harbinger of landscape transformation. As it thaws, it reshapes the very ground of the Arctic.

Notable Ice Ages

Huronian Ice Age: This ice age occurred approximately 2.4 to 2.1 billion years ago. Before the Huronian Ice Age, the Earth had a hot, greenhouse-like condition with high levels of CO_2. During the ice age, the Earth's surface probably froze solid. This ice age ended because of the increase in greenhouse gases produced by volcanic activity.

Cryogenian Ice Age: This ice age occurred between 720 to 635 million years ago. Prior to this ice age, the Earth was in a warm period with high levels of carbon dioxide. During the Cryogenian period, Earth experienced the most severe ice ages in its history, some suggest it may have been a so-called "Snowball Earth," where ice covered the planet from the poles to the tropics. The ice age ended due to intense volcanic activity which increased the quantity of CO_2, causing a greenhouse effect.

Andean-Saharan Ice Age: This took place approximately 460 to 430 million years ago during the Late Ordovician and the Silurian period. Before this, during the Middle Ordovician, the climate was warm and sea levels were high. The ice age occurred in the southern hemisphere and ended due to the increase in CO_2 levels from volcanic activities, leading to a warmer climate. Sharks date back to this period as do horseshoe crabs!

Karoo Ice Age: Occurred approximately 360 to 260 million years ago during the Late Carboniferous and Early Permian periods. The Earth was warm with large tropical swamps before this. During this ice age, ice covered the southern region of Gondwana. The ice age ended due to the accumulation of CO2 from widespread volcanic activities, leading to a warmer climate.

Quaternary Glaciation or Pleistocene Ice Age: This is the most recent ice age, which occurred from about 2.6 million years ago to 11,700 years ago. Before this, the Earth was in a warm period known as the Pliocene. During this ice age, massive ice sheets covered parts of North America, Northern Europe, and Asia. This ice age ended due to the changes in Earth's orbit and tilt, which affect the amount of sunlight reaching the Earth's surface, triggering a gradual warming trend.

Outrageous Ideas

Our understanding of when Ice Ages occurred is far more secure than our understanding of why they occurred. It is even less clear what caused an Ice Age to end. These theories are intriguing and often stimulate productive scientific debate, even if they're currently outside the mainstream. They also serve to remind us that our understanding of Earth's complex climate system and its history is still evolving, and there's much more to learn.

Pole Shift Theory: Charles Hapgood's pole shift theory, also known as Earth Crust Displacement theory, suggests that the Earth's outer crust can move rapidly over the mantle, causing the poles to shift significantly. This shift could potentially trigger an ice age by moving temperate regions to polar latitudes ... within hours.

Evidence: Hapgood pointed to the existence of maps like the Piri Reis Map, which he believed showed the Antarctic land mass as ice-free, implying a pole shift. He also cited the rapid and severe climate change found in the fossil record, for example, woolly mammoths found frozen with tropical vegetation in their mouths, evidence of a vast and swift change.

Counter Evidence: Mainstream science has yet to accept this theory. The forces required for such shifts far exceed what is considered geologically possible. However, it's important to distinguish this from the well-accepted phenomenon of 'polar wandering' due to plate tectonics, which is a slow, gradual, and continual process. Magnetic North is currently wandering at approximately 35 miles per year.

Magnetic Field Reversals and Ice Ages: Some theories suggest a connection between reversals in the Earth's magnetic field and ice ages. The idea is based on paleomagnetic data showing that these events may coincide temporally. It's hypothesized that a magnetic reversal could affect Earth's climate, potentially triggering an ice age. However, there's currently no widely accepted physical mechanism that connects these phenomena, and many scientists view the temporal association as likely coincidental. During this time Earth's magnetic field drops, leaving it with little protection from cosmic radiation. This unfiltered radiation from space causes ionization in the air particles in Earth's atmosphere, destroying the Ozone layer and triggering a ripple of climate change across the globe.

Evidence: Paleomagnetic data show that these events may coincide temporally, leading to the hypothesis that a magnetic field reversal could affect Earth's climate, potentially triggering an ice age. While a full pole flip is more rare, excursions--where the magnetic field drops significantly but not far enough to qualify as a full reversal--appear to happen regularly, approximately every 6000 years. Researchers have been able to create a detailed timescale of how Earth's atmosphere changed over these excursion events by analyzing rings in ancient trees. Using radiocarbon dating, a technique to date ancient relics or events, a team can track the changes in radiocarbon levels during the magnetic pole reversal. This data is charted alongside the trees' annual growth rings, which act as an accurate, natural timestamp.

Counter Evidence: Many scientists view the temporal association as likely coincidental. Additionally, the last complete magnetic reversal, the Brunhes-Matuyama reversal, occurred approximately 780,000 years ago, far from any major glaciation event.

Cosmic Catastrophes: Some theories propose that extraterrestrial events, like the impact of a large asteroid or comet, or a nearby supernova, could trigger an ice age. The idea is that such an event could throw up enough dust and debris to block sunlight, dramatically cooling the Earth.

Evidence: The Younger Dryas event, a sudden global cooling around 12,800 years ago, has been suggested to be due to a comet impact, as evidenced by a thin layer of impact proxies, including nano-diamonds, found at numerous sites across the globe.

Counter Evidence: The astronomical and geological evidence for such events coinciding with ice ages is scant. Disruption of the Atlantic Meridional Overturning Circulation (AMOC) posits that a massive influx of freshwater from the melting North American ice sheets from the end of the Pleistocene Ice Age into the North Atlantic Ocean disrupted the AMOC.

The AMOC is a major component of Earth's climate system, responsible for transporting warm water from the tropics towards the North Atlantic. This influx of freshwater is believed to have diluted the ocean's salinity, reducing its density and thereby weakening the AMOC. As a result, less warm water was transported northward, leading to a cooling of the Northern Hemisphere and triggering the Younger Dryas. The disruption of the AMOC due to freshwater influx remains the leading explanation among scientists. It highlights the intricate connections between Earth's various systems and how changes in one can have far-reaching impacts on global climate.

Solar Variability: While it's established that minor changes in solar radiation can affect Earth's climate, some theories suggest that more significant solar variability could trigger ice ages. However, the solar output appears to be remarkably stable over geological timescales, and while solar variability can influence climate over short periods, it's not considered a primary driver of ice ages in mainstream science.

Evidence: The Maunder Minimum, a period of low sunspot activity in the late 17th century, coincided with a part of the Little Ice Age, a period of cooler temperatures in the Northern Hemisphere. This suggests that changes in solar activity could have a significant impact on Earth's climate.

Counter Evidence: While solar variability can influence climate over short periods, there's currently no consensus in the scientific community that it could trigger an ice age. The Little Ice Age itself is not considered a true ice age.

Ancient Civilizations

"When something is important enough, you do it even if the odds are not in your favor."
~Elon Musk

Fun Facts

The Great Pyramid's Precision: The Great Pyramid of Giza was built with such precision that the four sides of its base have an average error of only 58 millimeters in length. Remarkably, this was achieved without modern technology!

Roman Concrete Mystery: Ancient Roman concrete has withstood the test of time, often surpassing modern concrete in durability. The secret lies in its unique mixture, which scientists are still trying to fully understand.

Mayan Chocolate Currency: The Maya civilization used cacao beans as currency. Yes, chocolate was money! They also played a crucial role in the discovery and cultivation of chocolate as we know it today.

Stonehenge Acoustics: Stonehenge, the mysterious prehistoric monument in England, has an amazing acoustic property. It's believed that the placement of stones creates a sound field akin to a concert hall.

Egyptian Dentistry: Ancient Egyptians were pioneers in dentistry. They used a form of toothpaste made from ingredients like eggshells and ashes, and even attempted dental surgeries.

Hanging Gardens Suspense: The Hanging Gardens of Babylon, one of the Seven Wonders of the Ancient World, may not have been in Babylon at all! Some theories suggest they were actually located in Nineveh.

Sumerian Beer Recipe: The world's oldest known recipe for beer comes from a 3900-year-old Sumerian poem honoring Ninkasi, the patron goddess of brewing.

The Nazca Lines' Enigma: In the Peruvian desert, the Nazca Lines, large geoglyphs carved into the ground, have puzzled scientists and historians. Created by the Nazca culture between 500 BCE and 500 CE, these lines form various shapes and designs, visible only from the air.

Chinese Seismoscope: In 132 AD, Zhang Heng, a Chinese scientist, invented the first seismoscope, an instrument to detect earthquakes. It was incredibly advanced for its time.

Incan Communication: The Inca civilization didn't have a written language but used a system of knotted strings called quipu for record-keeping and communication.

Phoenician Alphabet Revolution: The Phoenicians developed one of the first alphabets, which greatly influenced the development of modern scripts, including the Latin alphabet.

Greek Fire Mystery: Byzantines used a weapon called Greek Fire that could continue burning even on water. The exact composition remains a mystery to this day.

Viking Navigation: Vikings used sunstones, a type of crystal, to navigate the seas even on cloudy days. They could locate the sun's position by observing the sky through these crystals.

Ancient Egyptian Wigs: In ancient Egypt, both men and women wore wigs made from human hair or sheep's wool. These wigs were often styled elaborately.

Mohenjo-Daro's Urban Planning: The city of Mohenjo-Daro, part of the Indus Valley Civilization, had advanced urban planning, including the world's first known urban sanitation systems.

Aztec Floating Gardens: The Aztecs built chinampas, floating gardens, which were highly efficient agricultural islands used for crop cultivation. These floating gardens, built on the lakes of the Valley of Mexico, were a marvel of agricultural engineering and significantly boosted agricultural productivity.

Roman Floor Heating: The Romans had a type of central heating in their homes called hypocaust, where hot air circulated under the floors and in the walls.

The Flourishing of the Mali Empire: The Mali Empire, one of the richest and largest empires in African history, flourished in the 14th century. Renowned for its wealth, especially in gold, the empire was also a center of learning and culture. Its most famous ruler, Mansa Musa, is often regarded as one of the richest individuals in history amassing more wealth than Elon Musk and Jeff Bezos combined in today's dollars.

Spartan Cryptic Messages: Spartans used a device called a scytale to send secret messages during military campaigns. The message was only readable when wrapped around a rod of the same diameter.

Olmec Colossal Heads: The Olmecs of Mesoamerica created colossal stone heads, some weighing up to 50 tons. The transportation and carving methods are still subjects of awe and speculation.

Ancient Persian Refrigerators: Ancient Persians built structures called yakhchāls, which were early forms of refrigerators used to store ice and food.

Nabatean Water Technology: The Nabateans, builders of the city of Petra, were masters of water technology, creating an efficient system of dams, channels, and reservoirs in the desert.

Astronomical Alignment of Pyramids: The three pyramids of Giza are precisely aligned with the stars in the Orion's belt, showcasing the ancient Egyptians' advanced knowledge of astronomy.

Mayan Calendar Complexity: The Mayan calendar was so complex that it was more accurate than the Julian calendar used in Europe for centuries. Their Long Count calendar, which could predict celestial events thousands of years into the future, is a marvel of mathematical complexity.

Pompeii's Graffiti: In Pompeii, archaeologists have found ancient graffiti, providing insight into the daily life and thoughts of ordinary people.

Angkor Wat's Hydraulic System: Angkor Wat in Cambodia had an elaborate hydraulic system for irrigation and flood control, which was key to its prosperity.

Baghdad Battery Mystery: Objects known as the Baghdad Batteries, dating back to the Parthian period, suggest that ancient peoples might have had a form of galvanic electricity, though their true purpose remains a topic of debate and wonder.

Göbekli Tepe's Mysteries: Göbekli Tepe in modern-day Turkey predates Stonehenge by some 6,000 years dating back to 11,000 BCE. This site, with its carved stone megaliths arranged in circles, challenges our understanding of prehistoric societies. In the same region, Boncuklu Tarla was recently discovered to be at least 1,000 years older than Göbekli Tepe.

LIDAR's Revelation of Lost Civilizations: LIDAR technology uses light detection and ranging to map out the Earth's surface. Hidden beneath dense forests, LIDAR has uncovered extensive and sophisticated networks of cities, roads, and structures. These discoveries have reshaped our understanding of pre-Columbian societies, revealing them to be more populous, interconnected, and technologically advanced than previously thought.

Oxygen Threshold

To sustain human life as we know it, Earth's atmosphere needs to maintain a delicate balance, with oxygen levels ideally above 19.5%. Any lower, and human survival becomes increasingly challenging. This threshold sets a fascinating timeline in Earth's history:

- Before the Cambrian Explosion (about 541 million years ago): Oxygen levels were far below the minimum required for human life, hovering around 15% or less. This era, dominated by simple, mostly aquatic life forms, was an inhospitable period for any human-like species.
- The Cambrian Period and Beyond: Post-Cambrian Explosion, oxygen levels began a gradual ascent, paving the way for more complex life. However, it wasn't until around 400 million years ago, after the Devonian period, that oxygen levels consistently rose above the 19.5% mark.
- The Human-Compatible Window: The window for human-compatible oxygen levels opened up in the late Paleozoic era. From about 300 million years ago onwards, the atmosphere's oxygen concentration stabilized within a range suitable for human-like life forms, setting the stage for the eventual emergence of human ancestors in the geological timeline.

Ancestors

This list is a scratch on the surface of our brilliant human ancestry. Consider this a loving look back at what we have managed to figure out about our shared past and mostly what we have not.

Aboriginal Culture (65000 BCE - present): Around 65,000 years ago, the first Aboriginal ancestors arrived in Australia. This was the last Ice Age. Mammoths roamed the Earth, and vast ice sheets covered large parts of the globe. The Aboriginal peoples of Australia present a fascinating case study in long-term climate adaptation.

The Aboriginal rock art, some of the oldest globally, can be viewed as an ancient form of data recording. Where modern scientists use tools and databases to record observations, Aboriginal ancestors used rock art to document important events, animal species, environmental changes, and even the mundane.

Aboriginal spirituality, deeply intertwined with the land, saw the natural world as a living, breathing entity. Every mountain, river, and rock held significance. Fire-stick farming, practiced by the Aboriginal peoples, is a prime example of sustainable land management. By deliberately setting small fires, they controlled undergrowth and prevented larger, more destructive bushfires. This method of environmental stewardship offers parallels to contemporary controlled burning practices used in forestry management.

Jomon Culture (14000 BCE - 300 BCE): The Jomon people of Japan pioneered pottery production at a time when most of the world had not discovered this craft. Their pottery, dating as far back as 14,000 BCE, showcases an extraordinary level of sophistication. These pots were often decorated with intricate patterns, including cord markings (from which the term "Jomon," or "cord-patterned," derives). The designs weren't merely aesthetic; they indicated the pot's purpose – whether for cooking, storage, or rituals. The complexity of Jomon pottery can be compared to the early stages of the industrial revolution, where innovation transformed basic utility items into works of craftsmanship and technological marvels. Elements of Jomon culture, especially in pottery and art, have influenced contemporary Japanese culture. Some traditional Japanese pottery styles trace their origins back to Jomon techniques.

Apart from pottery, the Jomon people are known for their clay figurines, called "dogu." These figures, often female, are believed to have held spiritual significance, possibly used in rituals for fertility or healing. Certain spiritual and religious practices in modern Japan echo the animistic beliefs of the Jomon, reflecting a cultural continuity spanning thousands of years.

The Jomon built pit dwellings, semi-underground with thatched roofs, suggesting a semi-sedentary lifestyle. The size and number of dwellings in archaeological sites imply a clan-based society, where extended families likely lived in close proximity. This social structure can be likened to early forms of village communities seen in later civilizations.

Vinča Culture (5700 BCE - 4500 BCE): The Vinča Culture, thriving in what is now Serbia, represents a pinnacle of Neolithic Europe's societal development. Noted for their significant urban planning, the Vinča people developed some of the earliest large-scale settlements, indicative of a complex social structure. Their most prominent site, Vinča-Belo Brdo, reveals houses made of wattle and daub, arranged in a layout that suggests a high degree of organization and communal living.

One of the most striking aspects of the Vinča Culture is their proto-writing system. The symbols, found inscribed on pottery and figurines, exhibit a level of abstract thought that predates Mesopotamian cuneiform and Egyptian hieroglyphs. While the exact purpose of these symbols remains debated, ranging from religious to administrative uses, their sophistication underscores the Vinča's advanced cognitive abilities.

Economically, the Vinča were primarily agrarian, cultivating crops and domesticating animals, but they also engaged in significant trade. Their location in the Balkans provided a strategic trade route, facilitating exchanges with other cultures. This interaction likely spurred technological and cultural advancements.

Artistically, the Vinča people are known for their intricate figurines, often depicting human forms with stylized features. These artifacts, alongside decorative pottery, suggest a culture with a rich spiritual or religious life, although the specific beliefs and practices remain largely speculative.

The decline of the Vinča Culture is not entirely understood, but evidence points to a combination of climatic changes and the societal shifts associated with the advent of the Copper Age. This transition marked an evolution in technology and societal organization, leading into a new era of human development.

Sumerians (4500 BCE - 1900 BCE): delve into the world of the Sumerians and you'll discover a civilization that was not only advanced but transformative. They are celebrated for introducing the world to cuneiform, the earliest known form of writing. This breakthrough wasn't just about keeping records; it was a leap forward in communication, law, and literature. They brought us the wheel, revolutionizing transport and technology. Their ziggurats, towering structures reaching nearly 70 feet, like the famed Ziggurat of Ur, were not just religious centers but symbols of their architectural ingenuity, comparable in height to a modern seven-story building.

In cities like Uruk, possibly the world's first true city, and Ur, the Sumerians' urban planning and societal organization were ahead of their time. They practiced advanced agriculture, formulated complex mathematics, and laid down laws that predate Hammurabi's code. The decline of this civilization is a complex tapestry of causes. Ecological challenges such as soil salinization, a consequence of intensive agriculture, played a significant role. This environmental strain, coupled with internal strife and external pressures from invasions by groups like the Akkadians, gradually eroded the Sumerian civilization.

Norte Chico Civilization (3500 BCE - 1800 BCE): The Norte Chico civilization, flourished in present-day Peru, emerged from the shadows of the last Ice Age, not in the fertile river valleys of Mesopotamia or along the Nile, but in a coastal desert, an environment seemingly hostile to the grandeur civilizations are known for.

Architecturally, Norte Chico was a marvel of its time. The pyramids at Caral, their most iconic achievement, stand as silent witnesses to a forgotten world. These structures, some of the oldest known pyramids in the Americas, were not mere monuments; they were the heart of civic and religious life. Picture the scene: bustling activity as people gathered for ceremonies or to discuss the matters of their city, the pyramids looming large overhead, symbols of a collective strength.

But what truly sets Norte Chico apart is its subtlety in the artifacts left behind. There are no grand tombs or elaborate gold treasures. Instead, we find remnants of urban planning and textile fragments, suggesting a society that valued community and craftsmanship. The city layout indicates a complex understanding of urban spaces, with residential and public areas distinct yet interconnected, mirroring the intricate designs of their textiles.

Remarkably, Norte Chico's civilization developed independently of those in Mesopotamia, Egypt, India, and China. They achieved this without a known written language or the wheel, innovations typically associated with more advanced societies. Instead, their achievements in agriculture, evidenced by canal irrigation, sustained their cities and set the stage for later South American civilizations.

The decline of Norte Chico remains a mystery wrapped in the sands of time. There's no clear evidence of conquest or natural disaster. Perhaps, like many civilizations, it was a victim of its own success, its growth unsustainable in the harsh desert environment. Or maybe it slowly melded into the tapestry of Andean cultures that followed, leaving behind not a dramatic end, but a quiet transition.

The Indus Valley Civilization (3300 BCE - 1300 BCE): thriving in today's Pakistan and northwest India, stands out for its remarkable urban planning and architectural prowess. Cities like Mohenjo-Daro and Harappa showcased an urban design sophistication that parallels modern city planning. Their grid-patterned streets and advanced drainage systems, akin to contemporary sewage networks, reflect a deep understanding of urban infrastructure.

This civilization's mastery extended to hydraulic engineering, evident in the Harappan cities, where they developed the world's earliest known urban sanitation systems. These systems were not only functional but also ingeniously designed, showing parallels with the much later Roman aqueducts. The standardized weights and measures used across the civilization indicate a well-organized trade network and administrative system, comparable to the economic systems in modern nations.

Intriguingly, the civilization's script, found on numerous seals, remains undeciphered, presenting a puzzle as complex and alluring as the Rosetta Stone. The artifacts, including pottery and these seals, offer a glimpse into a culture rich in artistic expression and complexity.

The decline of this civilization is a subject of intense debate and speculation. One of the leading theories suggests a series of tectonic events, possibly earthquakes, that could have altered the course of the Indus River, undermining the agricultural and economic foundation of these cities. This theory is supported by geological evidence indicating significant shifts in the landscape during this period. Other theories range from Aryan invasions, reminiscent of the dramatic territorial wars of medieval times, to catastrophic climate change, which might have led to prolonged droughts or floods, disrupting the delicate balance of an agrarian society.

Minoan Civilization (2700 BCE - 1450 BCE): In the heart of the Mediterranean, nestled on the island of Crete, flourished the Minoan Civilization, a beacon of art, trade, and cultural sophistication. Knossos, the jewel in the Minoan crown, a palatial maze teeming with life and grandeur. Its complex architecture, with multistoried buildings, vibrant frescoes, and intricate drainage systems, speaks to a society far ahead of its time.

The Minoans left behind a legacy etched in clay and paint. Their frescoes are windows into their world, depicting lively scenes of bull-leaping, religious rites, and daily life with a vividness that almost seems to leap off the walls.

Equally enigmatic are the Linear A tablets, a linguistic puzzle that to this day defies deciphering. These tablets, inscribed with the earliest form of written Greek, suggest a complex administrative and trade network. The Minoans were not isolated artists; they were savvy traders who navigated the seas, exchanging goods and ideas with Egypt, the Near East, and mainland Greece.

The question of their decline, however, remains shrouded in mystery and speculation. Some point to the catastrophic eruption of Thera (modern-day Santorini), a volcanic event so massive it would have sent tidal waves crashing onto Crete, upending the Minoan way of life. Others suggest a more gradual decline, with the Mycenaeans from mainland Greece encroaching on Minoan territory, eventually absorbing or overpowering their culture.

Atlantis (Mythical): Atlantis, a name that echoes with the allure of mystery and the grandeur of a lost civilization, is a legend first breathed to life by the ancient Greek philosopher Plato in his dialogues "Timaeus" and "Critias." Described as a formidable naval power, Atlantis is said to have existed beyond the "Pillars of Hercules," and in a dramatic twist of fate, purportedly vanished beneath the ocean in a cataclysmic event of earthquakes and floods - all within the span of a single day and night.

The tale of Atlantis has captivated scholars, dreamers, and conspiracy theorists alike, inspiring a myriad of interpretations and debates. While mainstream history regards Atlantis as a myth or an allegory for the hubris of nations, the sheer detail in Plato's description has fueled endless speculation about its existence and location. Proposed sites for this enigmatic city range from the Mediterranean to the exotic depths of the Caribbean, and even to the icy fringes of Antarctica.

Adding to the mystique are fringe theories painting Atlantis not just as an advanced civilization of its time, but as a society possessing technology far beyond what was known to ancient humans. Some even venture into the realms of science fiction, suggesting extraterrestrial origins – a testament to the enduring human fascination with the unknown and the unexplained.

Among the more grounded theories is the hypothesis linking Atlantis to real historical societies. The Minoan civilization, for instance, with its advanced culture and sudden devastation by a volcanic eruption, is often cited as a possible real-world inspiration for the Atlantis myth. This theory posits that the story of Atlantis could be a distorted historical memory, passed down through generations and embellished into legend.

Despite extensive archaeological and geological explorations, no concrete evidence of Atlantis has been uncovered, leaving it to reside in the realm of speculation and folklore. The legend of Atlantis, with its blend of historical possibility and mythical grandeur, continues to spark the imagination and debate, inviting us to explore the tantalizing question: "What if?"

The Xia Dynasty (2070 BCE - 1600 BCE): The Xia Dynasty, emerging around 2070 BCE in what is now modern-day China, offers a captivating glimpse into the origins of one of the world's oldest civilizations. Often hailed as China's inaugural dynasty, the Xia blends the boundaries between myth and history, creating a tapestry of intrigue and cultural genesis.

At the heart of the Xia narrative are the tales and legends, primarily sourced from ancient texts like the Bamboo Annals. These chronicles paint a vivid picture of a society steeped in ritualistic practices, monarchial rule, and a strong connection with the natural world. The dynasty, purportedly founded by the legendary Yu the Great, was characterized by his heroic efforts in controlling the devastating floods that plagued the region. This tale, while partly mythological, resonates with themes of harmony between humanity and nature, a concept deeply ingrained in Chinese philosophy.

Archaeologically, the Xia remains elusive. The dearth of concrete evidence has led to spirited debates among historians and archaeologists, with some asserting its existence as purely mythical. However, recent excavations, such as those in Erlitou, suggest the presence of a sophisticated culture with bronze technology, urban planning, and social stratification, hinting at the possible reality of the Xia.

The decline of the Xia, shrouded in as much mystery as its existence, is often attributed to a combination of environmental disasters and internal strife. The narrative of a dynasty brought down by natural calamities intertwines with stories of moral decay and divine retribution, a common motif in ancient civilizations. The transition to the Shang Dynasty, marked by a more definitive historical footprint, signals the end of the Xia, but the dynasty's legacy in Chinese history is undiminished.

In the broader context of ancient civilizations, the Xia's story is not unique in its blend of myth and reality. Similar to the tales of Romulus and Remus in the founding of Rome, the Xia Dynasty serves as a foundational myth, a narrative crucial in shaping the cultural and historical identity of a people.

Ancient Nubia (c. 2000 BCE - 350 CE): This remarkable civilization, often overshadowed by its northern neighbor, Ancient Egypt, thrived in the region that is now Sudan, along the lush and life-giving Nile River Valley.

The Nubians were master builders, their legacy etched in the form of pyramids, albeit smaller and steeper than their Egyptian counterparts. These pyramids, primarily located in the ancient cities of Meroë, Kerma, and Napata, served as tombs for kings and queens, a testament to the sophisticated social hierarchy and religious beliefs that guided Nubian society. The Nubian pyramids, numbering over 200, stand as enduring symbols of a civilization deeply rooted in ritualistic and funerary traditions.

In the realm of writing, the Nubians developed their own script, known as Meroitic, around the 2nd century BCE. This script, still not fully deciphered, was used for both administrative and ceremonial purposes. The existence of Meroitic writing demonstrates the Nubians' advanced intellectual achievements and their unique cultural identity, distinct from their Egyptian neighbors.

Economically, Ancient Nubia was a powerhouse, leveraging its strategic location to become a hub of trade. Nubians traded gold, ivory, incense, and ebony with neighboring regions, including Egypt, the Middle East, and the Mediterranean, facilitating cultural exchange and economic prosperity.

The art and craft of Nubia were equally remarkable. Nubian pottery, known for its elegantly thin walls and distinctive, often geometric patterns, reflects a high level of artistic and technical skill. Their jewelry, made of gold and precious stones, exhibits fine craftsmanship and aesthetic sensibility.

The decline of Nubian civilization is a subject of historical speculation. Factors such as environmental changes, over-exploitation of resources, and external conflicts likely played a role. The shift in power dynamics with Egypt, particularly during periods of Egyptian conquest and Nubian independence, also significantly impacted the trajectory of Nubian history.

Maya Civilization (2000 BCE - 900 CE): Located in Mesoamerica, the Maya civilization is known for its hieroglyphic script, architecture, and astronomical system. Rooted in regions of modern-day Mexico, Belize, Guatemala, El Salvador, and Honduras, the Maya are celebrated for their profound contributions in various domains, including their intricate hieroglyphic script, monumental architecture, and advanced astronomical system.

Central to Maya achievement was their hieroglyphic writing, one of the most sophisticated in the pre-Columbian Americas. This script was not merely a means of record-keeping; it was a vessel carrying the complexities of their history, mythology, and rituals. The Maya codices, though few in number due to Spanish conquest efforts, provide invaluable insights into their society, including detailed astronomical observations and calendrical systems, showcasing a deep understanding of celestial mechanics.

Architecturally, the Maya were master builders, creating sprawling cities with grand pyramids, palaces, and plazas. Sites like Tikal and Chichen Itza stand as testaments to their engineering prowess. These urban centers were more than just population hubs; they were the epicenters of Maya religious, political, and cultural life. The precision of their construction, aligned with astronomical events, underscores the Maya's deep connection with the cosmos.

The decline of the Classic Maya Civilization around 900 CE is a subject of intense scholarly debate. Factors like overpopulation, environmental degradation, warfare, and political instability are often cited. Particularly compelling is the evidence of severe droughts, potentially exacerbated by deforestation and agricultural practices. These environmental stresses likely played a significant role in the fragmentation of their political systems and the abandonment of their great cities.

Yet, the end of the Classic period was not the end of Maya culture. Descendants of the ancient Maya continue to live in Mesoamerica, maintaining a rich tapestry of cultural practices, languages, and traditions. This enduring legacy is a testament to the resilience and adaptability of the Maya people through centuries of change.

In essence, the Maya Civilization offers a captivating story of human ingenuity, complex social organization, and profound interaction with the natural world, leaving a legacy that continues to fascinate and inform current generations.

The Lapita Culture (1600 BCE - 500 BCE): The Lapita Culture, emerging around 1600 BCE and fading by 500 BCE, played a pivotal role in the peopling of the Pacific Islands. Originating from Near Oceania, these skilled navigators and seafarers embarked on an expansive oceanic journey, reaching as far as Remote Oceania, which includes modern-day Polynesia, Micronesia, and parts of Melanesia.

The hallmark of the Lapita people is their distinctive pottery, characterized by intricate geometric designs. These designs, often stamped into the clay before firing, display a sophisticated level of artistic and technical skill. The widespread distribution of this pottery across the Pacific Islands serves as concrete evidence of the Lapita's extensive maritime exploration and settlement patterns.

Beyond their artistic legacy, the Lapita's greatest contribution is perhaps their navigational prowess. Using outrigger canoes capable of long-distance oceanic travel, they undertook some of the earliest known seafaring expeditions over vast expanses of the Pacific Ocean. This achievement is not merely a feat of physical endurance but also of navigational expertise, relying on knowledge of the stars, ocean currents, and wind patterns.

The Lapita were also accomplished agriculturalists and fishermen, adept at adapting to the varied environments of the Pacific Islands. Their settlements typically featured houses on stilts, indicative of a lifestyle attuned to the coastal and lagoon environments of the islands.

The gradual decline or transformation of the Lapita Culture is not marked by conquest or catastrophe but rather a seamless evolution into the diverse array of distinct island cultures that populate the Pacific today. This transition reflects a dynamic adaptation to local environments and resources, leading to the development of unique cultural and linguistic identities among the Pacific Islander populations.

In essence, the Lapita Culture embodies the human spirit of exploration and adaptation. Their legacy is etched not only in their pottery fragments but also in the genetic, linguistic, and cultural tapestry of the Pacific Island populations, a testament to their remarkable journey across the seas.

The Olmec Civilization (1200 BCE - 400 BCE): The Olmec Civilization, flourishing from 1200 BCE to 400 BCE in what is now Mexico, stands as a testament to the enigmatic grandeur of ancient Mesoamerica. These early trailblazers of civilization are celebrated for their mammoth stone heads, mysterious and commanding, which have puzzled and awed archaeologists and historians alike. Carved from single basalt boulders, these heads, some towering at over 9 feet tall and weighing several tons, are believed to represent rulers or important individuals, though their exact significance remains shrouded in the mists of time.

At the heart of Olmec society were bustling urban centers like La Venta and San Lorenzo. These were not just political hubs but also cradles of creativity and innovation. Here, the Olmecs pioneered advancements in architecture and urban planning, evident in their structured layouts and ceremonial complexes. Intriguingly, La Venta's layout appears aligned with magnetic north, hinting at a sophisticated understanding of Earth's geomagnetism.

Their sculptures and jade carvings depict a fascinating interplay of human and animalistic features, possibly reflecting religious or mythological beliefs. The Olmec art is characterized by its depiction of 'were-jaguars' – a fusion of human and jaguar characteristics, possibly symbolizing shamanistic transformations or a deep spiritual reverence for jaguars.

The Olmecs are also credited with laying the foundational cultural groundwork for later Mesoamerican civilizations, evident in shared iconography and religious motifs. This cultural continuity suggests a significant, if enigmatic, legacy that the Olmecs left behind.

However, the curtain fell on this remarkable civilization around 400 BCE. Theories abound about their decline, ranging from environmental catastrophes like volcanic eruptions and flooding to internal social strife and overexploitation of resources. The collapse of the Olmecs marks a poignant chapter in Mesoamerican history, an early rise and fall that set the stage for the civilizations that followed.

Great Zimbabwe (1100 CE - 1450 CE): Great Zimbabwe, in what is now modern-day Zimbabwe, stands as a monumental testament to the architectural and economic prowess of ancient African civilizations. This society, primarily recognized for its majestic stone structures, provides insight into a sophisticated and prosperous society.

The central feature of Great Zimbabwe is its impressive stone complexes, built without mortar yet standing robustly to this day. The most iconic among these is the Great Enclosure, featuring walls over 16 feet (5 meters) high and extending over 800 feet (250 meters), making it the largest ancient structure in Sub-Saharan Africa. These structures, often referred to as Zimbabwe Ruins, demonstrate a high level of craftsmanship and are believed to have served various functions, from religious to administrative.

Economically, Great Zimbabwe was a nexus of regional trade, significantly propelled by cattle herding and gold trade. Evidence suggests that cattle were a crucial economic and social asset, likely used as a measure of wealth and in trade exchanges. The region's abundant gold resources played a pivotal role in establishing Great Zimbabwe as a trading powerhouse, engaging in far-reaching trade networks that extended to the Indian Ocean coast.

Culturally, the civilization is thought to have been complex and hierarchical, as indicated by the scale and design of their structures. Artifacts such as pottery, jewelry, and imported items like Chinese porcelain and Arabian glassware found at the site indicate a cosmopolitan society engaged in extensive trade networks.

The decline of Great Zimbabwe around the mid-15th century CE is largely attributed to ecological factors. Overgrazing, coupled with climatic changes, likely led to a depletion of resources necessary to sustain the large population. This environmental degradation, compounded by the pressure of a growing population, may have prompted the inhabitants to migrate to more fertile lands, leading to a gradual abandonment of the site.

Rapa Nui (1200 CE -): a speck in the vast Pacific Ocean, Easter Island holds an enthralling tale of human ingenuity and mystery. The island's first inhabitants, believed to have arrived around 1200 CE, hailed from East Polynesia. Their journey across the ocean is a testament to their remarkable navigational skills and adventurous spirit.

The most striking legacy they left behind are the Moai, majestic stone statues that have captivated the world's imagination. Recent archaeological excavations have unveiled startling revelations about these iconic figures. Far more than just heads, many of the Moai are intricately carved full-bodies sculpted with detailed torsos, extending deep underground. This discovery has reshaped our understanding of the Rapa Nui people's artistic and engineering prowess. Recent archaeological work has also provided more insights into the Rapa Nui people's sophisticated agricultural practices, including the use of rock gardens and advanced soil management, which challenges earlier notions of ecological collapse.

Outrageous Ideas

Consider the architectural wonders of our ancient world - the pyramids of Egypt, the enigmatic Stonehenge, and the precise Nazca Lines. These feats may not be products of human ingenuity but rather were helped along by something not of this world. The complexity and astronomical alignments of these structures hint at knowledge and technology that could have been imparted by visitors, far surpassing what was thought possible for our Earth-grown ancient civilizations.

Current accepted explanations for human development cannot explain the remarkable and somewhat mysterious acceleration in human brain development and cognitive abilities we find in the fossil record. This sudden leap, particularly in the size and complexity of the human brain, is seen as too rapid to be solely a product of natural evolution. Between 800,000 and 200,000 years ago, Homo sapiens experienced a significant increase in brain volume. The average human brain size expanded from about 600 cubic centimeters to nearly 1500 cubic centimeters. This rapid expansion in brain capacity, particularly when compared to the much slower rate of brain growth in other species, may point to external intervention, a nudge in our evolutionary journey.

Some believe we were visited by people who may have arrived here by the moon. This is wild speculation, but the Spaceship Moon fans point to many issues with both our evolutionary record and our societal records. Across different cultures and eras, ancient artwork and mythologies frequently depict celestial themes, often featuring the moon prominently. Cave paintings, ancient carvings, and religious texts from around the world showcase figures or objects descending from the sky, interpreted as representations of lunar beings interacting with early humans. These are not dismissed as mere myths or artistic expressions but are considered to be historical records of extraterrestrial contact by some.

- The cave paintings in Tassili n'Ajjer in Algeria, estimated to be up to 12,000 years old, feature figures that appear to be wearing space suits or helmets, which some interpret as depictions of extraterrestrial beings.
- In ancient Sumerian mythology, the deity Enki, who was associated with creation and intelligence, is often linked to the moon. The detailed accounts of Enki in the Sumerian texts are viewed by some as records of an extraterrestrial being from the moon influencing human development.
- The Dogon people of Mali have traditional beliefs that revolve around the Sirius star system, but also include detailed knowledge of the moon. Their mythologies speak of ancestral beings called Nommo, described as amphibious beings from the sky. Proponents of the theory argue that the Dogon's advanced astronomical knowledge, which includes detailed understanding of lunar cycles, could have been imparted by lunar visitors.

The precision and astronomical alignment of structures like the Great Pyramid of Giza are also often cited. The pyramid's orientation to the cardinal points, its alignment with the Orion's Belt, and the remarkable accuracy in its construction are presented as beyond the capabilities of the ancient Egyptians without external assistance. Many point to far more recent inhabitants in Egypt to emphasize the point emphasizing delayed ability to provide clean drinking water. The disparity between the phenomenal engineering precision of much earlier Egyptians and the less capable modern counterparts is enough to fuel the theory of early assistance. Perhaps lunar beings, with advanced knowledge of astronomy and engineering, played a role in guiding the construction of these monumental structures.

It is the cave art minus the moon that strengthens the argument for others. Prehistoric cave art reveals that ancient humans had a complex understanding of astronomy as far back as 40,000 years ago. Cave art across Europe features animal symbols that represent star constellations, used to mark events like comet strikes. This includes the Lascaux Shaft Scene in France, thought to commemorate a comet strike around 15,200 BC. This famous artwork in the Lascaux Caves features a dying man and several animals. The representation of the comet strike in this artwork aligns with the advanced astronomical knowledge possessed by the people of that era. Constellations point us to specific knowledge of star alignment at the time ... but no moon. The caves do not appear to show a moon for Earth. Even further back, dated to 40,000 years ago, the Lion-Man of Hohlenstein-Stadel Cave, Germany is the world's oldest known sculpture and conforms to the ancient time-keeping system based on astronomical observations. This sculpture is considered an early representation of the Leo zodiac sign, suggesting a connection to the constellations. This absence of the moon is notable considering the otherwise rich and diverse array of subjects covered in these ancient artworks and celestial observation.

The moon itself is an enigma, with peculiarities in its composition and orbit. Some point to these anomalies as evidence of the moon's artificial nature, suggesting it was strategically placed in Earth's orbit by advanced beings. The moon's influence on Earth's tides and its role in creating stable conditions for life is seen not as coincidental but as part of a deliberate design.

> *"Absence of evidence is not the*
> *evidence of absence."*
> *~Carl Sagan*

Humans

"We meet no ordinary people in our lives."
~C.S. Lewis

Fun Facts

Blinking Symphony: On average, a person blinks about 15-20 times per minute. That's up to 1,200 times an hour and a staggering 28,800 times a day!

Stomach's Acidic Power: Your stomach acid is strong enough to dissolve metal. It needs to be this powerful to break down food, but don't worry – the stomach lining renews itself frequently to prevent damage.

The Unbeatable Heart: Over an average lifetime, the human heart beats more than 2.5 billion times, tirelessly pumping millions of gallons of blood throughout the body.

Bone Strength Surprises: Human bones are incredibly strong. Ounce for ounce, they are stronger than steel and can bear a load of around 19,000 lbs (8,626 kg) which is roughly the weight of five pickup trucks!

The Amazing Brain: The human brain can generate about 23 watts of power – enough to power a small light bulb.

Super Skin: Skin is the body's largest organ. If stretched out, the skin of an average adult would cover 22 square feet.

Lung Expansions: The total length of airways running through your lungs is about 1,500 miles, roughly the distance from Chicago to Santa Fe.

Hair's Prolific Growth: Hair grows slightly faster in warm weather because heat stimulates circulation and encourages hair growth.

The Blood Highway: If laid end to end, an adult's blood vessels could circle Earth's equator four times!

Eye's Colorful World: Human eyes can distinguish between approximately 10 million different colors.

The Microbial Universe Within: Your body houses 10 times more bacterial cells than human cells. This bustling microbiome is essential for digestion, immunity, and even affects mood and behavior.

Nail Growth Mysteries: Fingernails grow faster on your dominant hand. If you're right-handed, your right hand's nails grow faster and vice versa.

Sneezing Speeds: A sneeze can exit the body at speeds up to 100 miles per hour!

Taste Bud Lifespan: Taste buds have a life cycle of about 10 days. They're constantly renewing to keep your sense of taste sharp.

The Unparalleled Liver: The liver is a multitasking marvel. It impacts over 500 vital functions, including detoxification, protein synthesis, and digestion.

Brain's Water Content: Your brain is about 75% water, and dehydration can affect cognitive functions and mood.

Kidneys' Daily Filtration: Each day, your kidneys filter around 120-150 quarts of blood to produce about 1-2 quarts of urine, composed of wastes and extra fluid.

The Eye's Rapid Movements: Eyes can move 900 times an hour during reading – a workout for those tiny muscles!

Ear's Bone Evolution: The smallest bone in your body, the stapes in your ear, started evolutionarily as a gill bar in fish.

Unique Fingerprints: No two people have the same set of fingerprints, not even identical twins, making them a unique identifier.

Pregnancy Organ Growth: During pregnancy, a woman's uterus expands up to 500 times its normal size.

The Body's Cooling System: Humans have 2-4 million sweat glands. They work as a natural air conditioner to keep your body cool.

Facial Expression Muscles: It takes 43 muscles to frown but only 17 to smile – so smiling is literally the easier option!

Body Heat Production: The human body generates enough heat in just 30 minutes to boil half a gallon of water.

The Invisible Eyelash Mites: Almost everyone has tiny mites living in their eyelashes. These microscopic creatures are generally harmless and are part of the skin's natural flora.

Generations

Commonly, generations have been defined by chronological time periods, often spanning about 15-20 years. But it makes more sense to characterize each generation – Baby Boomers, Generation X, Millennials, and so forth – by the unique technological, cultural, social, and political events of their formative years. This method of categorization captures the collective experiences that shape a generation's values and outlook and accounts for some of the oddballs ahead of their time.

Consider the seismic shift brought about by the personal cell phone. For generations accustomed to landlines, the phone was a tether to a place – a household, an office. You called a location, hoping to reach a person. This mode of communication fostered a sense of communal interaction; the phone was a shared family resource, and conversations were often public, taking place in communal spaces.

Enter the era of personal cell phones, and the paradigm shifts dramatically. For those who came of age with a cell phone, having his or her own phone by age 15 – typically the Millennials and Generation Z – the phone became a personal portal, a direct line not to a place, but to an individual. This marks a profound change in the concept of communication and self-identity. When someone calls your cell phone, they're seeking you specifically, affirming your individuality and importance. This personalization of communication technology fosters a sense of independence and self-centrality from a young age.

This shift also transforms the nature of interaction. With landlines, the ringing phone demanded immediate attention, creating a reflex to respond to external stimuli. In contrast, cell phones allow for control over communication; one can choose when to engage or disconnect, shaping a generation more accustomed to managing their social interactions according to their schedule and preferences.

In terms of family dynamics, technology has played a subtle yet significant role. Traditional family units, often larger and multi-generational, were the norm in earlier generations. Shared landlines meant communication was a family affair, with everyone potentially involved or aware of the ongoing conversations. This setup reinforced a sense of collective family identity.

With the advent of personal cell phones, the dynamics have shifted. Communication has become more individual-centric. Younger generations experience a greater sense of agency in their interactions.

Looking at generations holistically, we see that technological advances like the cell phone don't just change how we talk; they reshape how we think about ourselves, our relationships, and our place in the world. It's not just about calling a person instead of a place; it's about the emergence of a more individualized, schedule-driven, and personal worldview.

Y Start Here?

Picture this tiny Y chromosome, often overshadowed by its robust partner, the X chromosome, as a character with a rich, albeit tumultuous, history. The Y has undergone a dramatic transformation over the past 180 million years. Unlike the X, which has maintained its genetic integrity, the Y has stopped recombining and embarked on a path of genetic decay. This diminutive chromosome, having lost 97% of its ancestral genes, now stands as a mere shadow of its former self, a testament to the relentless march of evolutionary change.

As the existence of female mammals shows, the shrunken Y doesn't contain any crucial genes, so cells and individuals can survive its loss. Indeed, recent studies show it is often lost from cells as men age. Overzealous speculators have postulated that the loss of the Y from an entire population should result in extinction. But not so fast.

Most chromosomes come in pairs, and each member of the pair contains pretty much the same information, give or take a few mutations or variations. To make an egg or sperm cell, a germ cell has to halve the number of chromosomes it has; in humans a normal cell has 46 chromosomes whereas an egg or sperm cell has only 23. This is meiosis. But the cell doesn't just pick one chromosome out of each pair and throw away the other. First it goes through a process called genetic recombination where enzymes cut up the DNA to swap pieces of DNA between the pair of chromosomes, creating two new chromosomes with completely new combinations of genes.

This process is super important at weeding out harmful mutations. Imagine if you had a hand of cards with some really good cards and some really bad cards, overall it would average out and maybe you would win your game with it, maybe you wouldn't. But if you shuffled your hand with the deck and now had a hand of all really bad cards, you'd definitely lose your card game so that whole hand would be eliminated. Genetic recombination allows harmful mutations to be exposed to the game of natural selection, so they can be weeded out when they're so harmful that the individual can't survive or reproduce.

The Y chromosome, however, can't go through this process. The Y chromosome doesn't contain the same genes as the X chromosome with a few mutations here and there, it contains completely different genes. When two Xs get together in someone with XX chromosomes, they can recombine to get rid of the bad genes. They average things out or they select the better copy - it isn't clear which or why. But because YY chromosome pairings are scarce, the poor old Y never gets the chance to dump all its bad mutations. It just accumulates and accumulates mutations until the genes are rendered completely useless and eventually disappear entirely.

And it's not just that the Y can't get rid of mutations, it also accumulates them more quickly. Whereas females are born with all the eggs they can produce, males continuously produce sperm cells throughout their life, meaning cells in the testes are continuously dividing and dividing, each time opening up the possibility of generating a new mutation. Since the Y chromosome can only be inherited through sperm, they're much more likely to be subject to this higher mutation rate.

With the double whammy of collecting more mutations and not being able to get rid of them, it's not ridiculous to suggest that the Y chromosome might eventually become so mutation-addled that it disappears entirely. In fact, it's already happened in other mammals, specifically the Amami spiny rat. These rats don't have a Y chromosome. They used to, 2 million years ago, but now it's gone. Both females and males have just one X chromosome. Even without sex chromosomes, there are still males and females. So, how?

The male rats have a duplicated region right next to a gene called SOX9 on one copy of their chromosome 3, but only one of the pair of chromosomes has this duplication. The SOX9 gene happens to be one of the key genes that the SRY, Sex-determining Region Y, region activates when it's barking its orders to masculinize the embryo, telling the embryo to grow testes.

The duplicated region next to the SOX9 gene boosts the activity of SOX9, which means it has the exact same effect that the SRY gene has in triggering testes development. Two different parts of the genome, same result. If you're a spiny rat and you inherit a copy of chromosome 3 with the duplication, you're a male. If neither of your chromosome 3s have the duplication, you're a female.

In humans, the Y chromosome is less than one-fifth the size of the X and has shed most of its original gene content, however, it still carries the crucial SRY gene, the master switch for male development in the embryo. About 12 weeks after conception, this gene's activation triggers a cascade of genetic events, leading to the formation of testes and the release of male hormones.

But here's the twist: the Y chromosome is slowly shrinking over time, sparking a lively scientific debate. Will it vanish entirely in humans, or will nature find a workaround? Is the Y chromosome even necessary?

It appears nature already has a workaround of sorts. Think of the SRY gene as the off-road package when you buy a new truck. When you select the off-road package, certain things are automatically added to the truck: 4-wheel drive, mud flaps, off-road tires, towing package, etc. You can usually get each of those options by adding them individually, but some benefits only come with getting the full package together. The X chromosome carries most of the individual options that the SRY gene triggers on the Y chromosome. They just require a different cascade of proteins to trigger the individual genes to match the elegance of the SRY gene. As a consequence it appears that the masculinization of the embryo can happen without requiring a Y chromosome though the Y chromosome with the SRY gene makes the process more clear. In some cases the SRY gene has been found on an X chromosome which led to a male fetus despite no Y chromosome. So we know it is possible to still have a masculine fetus without the Y chromosome.

The Y chromosome, with its modest collection of approximately 55 genes, is mostly composed of non-coding DNA. This stark difference in genetic content compared to the over 900 genes in the X sets the stage for a fascinating biological interplay.

In this genetic lottery, females, with their two X chromosomes, experience a unique form of genetic averaging. Imagine each X chromosome as a deck of cards; females shuffle two decks together, creating a blend of traits. For traits linked to the X chromosome, such as mitochondrial DNA, which fuels the development of and then functioning of the brain, this means that girls have two sets of genes that contribute to these abilities. If one X carries a less advantageous version of these genes, the other X can compensate, potentially leading to a more balanced expression of these traits.

Boys, on the other hand, play a high-stakes game with just one X chromosome, one deck of cards. Without a second X to balance the equation, boys face the extremes of the traits carried on their single X. This can lead to a 'hit or miss' scenario in traits like intelligence. If the X chromosome carries genes favorable to cognitive abilities, it shines through unchallenged. But if it carries less advantageous versions, there's no genetic safety net to fall back on.

Outrageous Ideas

Visualize the brain as a complex city, with its various regions functioning like distinct districts, each playing a crucial role in the realm of morality. In this neural metropolis, the frontal lobe, particularly the orbital and ventromedial prefrontal cortices, operates like the mayor's office. This critical district governs moral decision-making and emotional regulation. Neuroscientific studies have pinpointed how damage to this area can lead to impaired moral judgments and emotional dysregulation, underscoring its pivotal role in ethical behavior.

The temporal lobe, on the other hand, mirrors the city's social hub. Key areas like the superior temporal sulcus and the temporo-parietal junction thrive in understanding and interpreting others' intentions and beliefs. These regions are essential for complex moral decision-making, where understanding social cues and empathy plays a crucial role. Dysfunctions in this 'social district' of our brain city can lead to aggressive behavior or social misinterpretation, highlighting its importance in moral narratives.

Deep within the brain's intricate urban landscape lies the amygdala, akin to a central marketplace bustling with moral emotions. This region is pivotal in processing emotions crucial for moral judgments, such as fear and aggression. When the amygdala's balance is disturbed, it can lead to heightened aggression or impaired judgment, reflecting its role as the city's emotional epicenter.

Turning to the tools used to explore this neural city, fMRI scans act as high-tech surveillance systems, offering insights into the brain's activity during moral judgments. These scans reveal how regions like the medial prefrontal cortex and temporoparietal junction are engaged when making ethical decisions. Recent advancements in machine learning have even enabled the decoding of specific moral judgments based on brain activity patterns, highlighting the distinct neural pathways activated by different moral scenarios.

Researchers, guided by Moral Foundations Theory, have mapped the neural basis of morality within this brain city. This theory posits innate moral foundations categorized into individualizing foundations like care/harm and fairness/cheating and binding foundations like loyalty/betrayal and authority/subversion. Neuroimaging studies have identified specific brain activations associated with these foundations, revealing a diverse array of moral reasoning pathways within our cerebral cityscape.

Despite the uniqueness of each individual's moral compass, shaped by personal experiences and cultural background, there are universal moral principles that resonate across the human spectrum. These include altruism, fairness, respect for authority, and property rights, reflecting a shared moral frequency across humanity's diverse population.

Ethics are not just abstract concepts but tangible patterns of neural activity. Morality, in this light, emerges not only as a philosophical or cultural construct but as a fundamental aspect of our neurological makeup, a testament to the wonder and complexity of the human brain.

Engineering Marvels

*"We build too many walls and not
enough bridges."*
~Isaac Newton

Fun Facts

Mitsubishi Electric's Spiral Escalators: Mitsubishi Electric stands alone in the world for manufacturing spiral escalators. These engineering marvels offer a unique, almost cinematic experience, gracefully curving upwards with a vertical rise of up to 21 feet 7 inches.

Not just aesthetically pleasing, these escalators match the lifecycle of their straight counterparts and feature advanced control systems that adapt to changing traffic patterns. With just over 100 installed globally, why aren't these visually striking escalators more common?

Wireless Electricity: Imagine charging devices without cords. Wireless electricity transmission, a concept initially proposed by Nikola Tesla, is now becoming a reality with technologies that can power devices over short distances without direct contact.

3D Printers: 3D printing technology, once a sci-fi dream in shows like "Star Trek: The Next Generation" with the Replicator, is now a stunning reality. While we can't yet print a bowl of macaroni and cheese, today's 3D printers are creating space tools, model body organs, and more, pushing the boundaries of manufacturing and medical science and soon, food science!

Hover Bikes: Inspired by the iconic speeders from "Star Wars: Episode VI – Return of the Jedi," hover bikes have shifted from fantasy to reality. Post-2014 has seen a surge in these helicopter-like vehicles, sparking excitement and new possibilities in personal transportation.

Video Calls: The idea of video calling, popularized by 'The Jetsons' in the 1960s, has transitioned from a fanciful cartoon concept to an essential communication tool in our daily lives with technologies like Skype, FaceTime and the COVID era darling, Zoom!

Driverless Cars: The journey of driverless cars, from a speculative concept to reality, mirrors their portrayal in the 2002 film "Minority Report." Originating in the 1980s at Carnegie Mellon University, autonomous vehicles are now being developed by numerous companies, edging closer to becoming an everyday reality.

Smart Watches: The smartwatch, now a staple in wearable technology, was first conceptualized in the "Dick Tracy" comic strip in 1946. This early depiction of a two-way wrist radio, and later a video watch, predates modern smartwatches and reflects the longstanding human fascination with portable communication devices.

3D Holograms: The iconic holographic message from Princess Leia in "Star Wars" has inspired real-world holography. Today, holograms are used in various applications, from entertainment to retail, and have even been used to bring musical legends like Buddy Holly and Roy Orbison to the stage posthumously.

Biometric Devices: Biometric recognition has now become integral to security and personal device access, underlining the rapid evolution of technology from science fiction to essential security tools.

Hands-Free Gaming Consoles: "Back to the Future" humorously predicted hands-free gaming, a concept that seemed far-fetched at the time but is now realized in motion-sensing gaming technologies, reshaping the way we interact with virtual worlds.

Smart Clothing and Wearable Technology: The realm of smart clothing is rapidly expanding. Today's wearable tech includes fitness trackers, smart shirts monitoring vital signs, and baby onesies doubling as monitors. Emerging technologies like stain-proof clothes and color-changing heels are on the horizon, promising a future where clothing is as smart as our devices.

The Bionic Eye: Engineers have developed a 'bionic eye' that can restore sight to the blind. Using a tiny camera attached to glasses, the system sends signals directly to the optic nerve, offering hope to those with vision loss.

The Millau Viaduct: In France, the Millau Viaduct is a structural wonder, soaring 1,125 feet above the Tarn River Valley. It's taller than the Eiffel Tower, making it the tallest bridge in the world, a stunning blend of engineering and aesthetics.

Chemical Color Change: Did you know there's a building that changes color based on the air quality? The 'Torre de Especialidades' in Mexico City is coated in a special chemical that reacts to pollution, visually indicating air quality by changing colors.

The Soundless Room: The world's quietest place is at Orfield Laboratories in Minnesota. This anechoic chamber absorbs over 99% of sound, creating such a silent environment that you can hear your own heartbeat!

Solar Roads: In France, there's a road made of solar panels. The Wattway, a one-kilometer route, is an experiment in converting everyday infrastructure into renewable energy sources, showcasing how roads can do more than just support vehicles.

Artificial Photosynthesis: Scientists have developed a system for artificial photosynthesis, using sunlight to convert water and carbon dioxide into fuel. This technology mimics plants and could revolutionize renewable energy sources.

The Robot Swarm: Inspired by nature, engineers have created swarms of tiny robots that can work together to complete complex tasks. These robot swarms, mimicking the collective behavior of insects, represent a breakthrough in robotics and could be used in disaster relief and exploration.

The Flying Train: In China, researchers are developing a flying train that could travel up to 2,500 miles (4,000 kilometers) per hour. This ultra-fast train would use magnetic levitation and vacuum tubes to reduce air resistance, potentially revolutionizing long-distance travel.

Graphene Wonder Material: Graphene, a material just one atom thick, is stronger than steel and more conductive than copper. It's revolutionizing fields from electronics to medicine, with potential applications including ultra-fast electronics, water filtration systems, and even medical devices.

Self-Healing Concrete: Engineers have developed concrete that can heal its own cracks using bacteria. When water seeps into cracks, the bacteria activate and produce limestone, effectively sealing the crack and prolonging the structure's life.

The Earthquake-Proof Tower: Tokyo's Skytree, the world's tallest tower, is designed to withstand strong earthquakes. Its central shaft of reinforced concrete and unique design can absorb seismic energy, ensuring its stability amidst Japan's frequent earthquakes.

Space Construction

Sky-High Dreams: The Tower to Space: Ever thought of building a tower to space? It sounds like a fairy tale, but it's a scientific puzzle! Scientists estimate that space begins somewhere between 50 to 60 miles (80 to 100 kilometers) above Earth. Building a tower that tall, however, would be like stacking an impossibly high pile of Lego bricks. Eventually, it would lean, sway, and dramatically scatter its pieces across the cosmic stage. A pyramid-shaped structure might fare better, but it's still a fanciful thought in our grand cosmic construction plan.

Zero Gravity: A Cosmic Construction Conundrum: Imagine trying to build a sandcastle in a pool where the sand refuses to stay put. That's a bit like construction in outer space! Without gravity, the familiar laws of physics we rely on Earth go topsy-turvy. Traditional construction tools like cranes and cement mixers are stars of the earthbound building site, but in the zero-gravity ballet of space, they become cosmic comedians, utterly puzzled by their weightless stage.

The 3D Printing Puzzle: Creating in a Gravity-Free Dance: 3D printers, those magical machines that conjure objects out of seemingly thin air, face their own space oddity. On Earth, gravity is the invisible hand that guides each layer of a 3D printed object, ensuring it sticks and sets correctly. But in the vastness of space, without gravity's gentle touch, 3D printed creations can end up more abstract art than functional part, whimsically floating away before they can even dry!

Archinaut: The Cosmic Builder: Enter Archinaut, a space construction visionary. This incredible technology marries a "gravity-independent 3D printing technology" with flexible robotic arms, all aboard a single spacecraft. Archinaut could be the ultimate cosmic handyman, capable of constructing new structures in the void or repairing and upgrading celestial old-timers like satellites. It's like having a cosmic 3D printing wizard and robotic sorcerer working hand in hand, high above Earth creating large structures for space in space.

Crafting a Space Colony: The Ultimate Cosmic Challenge:
Building a space station colony is like putting together the most complex jigsaw puzzle in the galaxy. Supplies for this colossal endeavor might not all come from Earth. The moon and asteroids could be cosmic quarries, offering the building blocks for this space megastructure. However, moving these heavy materials into orbit presents a propulsion puzzle, a challenge that might one day be solved by futuristic nuclear rockets or an even more advanced system. And then there's the need for a closed-loop life support system – a space-age recycling wizard that transforms waste back into water and other essentials. The International Space Station is already dabbling in this cosmic recycling, but for a full-fledged colony, we'll need to turn it up a notch.

In the fantastical realm of outer space construction, every challenge is an opportunity for innovation and whimsy. From gravity-defying building techniques to interstellar resource gathering, the quest to build among the stars is a thrilling blend of science, imagination, and cosmic ambition. It's a testament to human ingenuity and our unending desire to reach for the stars and beyond.

Aquatic Living

Setting Sail for Undersea Settlements: Imagine packing your bags for a journey not to a distant planet, but to an underwater paradise. The idea isn't as far-fetched as it might seem. With Earth's surface being 71% water, envisioning the ocean as a new frontier for human habitation is a tantalizing prospect. The ocean, with its mysterious depths and vast expanse, offers a canvas for future generations to paint their aquatic dreams.

The Challenges of Subaquatic Architecture: Building beneath the waves presents a sea of challenges – from the bone-chilling cold and crushing pressure to the scarcity of oxygen. Living underwater could also have some quirky side effects on the human body. The architecture of such settlements would need to withstand immense pressures, especially beyond 1,000 feet (300 meters) deep, where the walls would need to be extraordinarily thick, and returning to the surface would require lengthy decompression stops.

Breathing Easy Under the Sea: Breathing underwater isn't as simple as on land. At depth, the human body needs a carefully balanced cocktail of gases. While plants and artificial lighting could supply some oxygen, managing levels of nitrogen or helium becomes crucial. Picture a world where your air isn't just a given but a complex, life-sustaining recipe!

- Effects of Extreme Atmospheric Pressure: Living under the sea alters the partial pressure of oxygen in the human body. This can have various physiological impacts, although the exact nature of these effects is still being studied. The research in this area is relatively limited, but it's known that technical saturation divers, who work at depths of up to 1,000 feet, often experience headaches, fatigue, and other ailments even when following proper protocols.
- Skin Infections or Rashes: Living in an underwater environment, such as a cabin or pod, can often lead to superficial skin infections or rashes. This is due to factors like the lack of sunlight, high humidity, and limited sanitary conditions in the environment. These conditions can become dangerous if not treated properly.

- Changes in Sleep Patterns and Physical Health: Joseph Dituri, who spent 100 days living underwater, reported experiencing more REM and deep sleep during his rest. He also noted improvements in his cholesterol and stress levels while living at depth. However, he emerged from his underwater stay slightly shorter in height and with worsened eyesight (myopia), likely due to the pressurized environment.

Materials and Techniques for Underwater Construction: When it comes to building materials, we need stuff that's not just strong but also resistant to corrosion by saltwater. Specialized concrete and glass, along with corrosion-resistant metals like titanium, could be key players in underwater construction. As for techniques, imagine large sections of buildings being constructed on land, then sunk and anchored to the ocean floor, akin to an underwater LEGO assembly.

Pioneering Underwater Structures: There are already several awe-inspiring underwater structures that hint at what future underwater cities could look like. From the Aquarius Reef Base, a scientific research facility off the coast of Florida, to the mesmerizing underwater hotels like the Conrad Maldives Rangali Island, these structures offer a glimpse into the potential of subaquatic living. Each one is a testament to human ingenuity – a blend of science and art, submerged in the deep blue.

Visionaries of the Deep: The Ocean Spiral City: Enter the architects of the Shimizu Corporation, who are not just dreaming but designing an ambitious $26 billion project to create an underwater city, the Ocean Spiral City. Envisioned off the coast of Tokyo, this futuristic city would power itself through the energy of waves, tides, and ocean currents. The plan includes accommodations for 5,000 people, complete with labs, schools, and residential areas – a thriving underwater community, expected to turn from dream to reality by 2030.

Outrageous Ideas

Embarking on a journey to construct in the realms beyond our traditional habitat, be it the cosmic void of space or the mysterious depths of our oceans, is an endeavor that tickles the imagination and challenges the boundaries of engineering and science. But which one would be easier?

Building in Space: The Final Frontier
Pros:

Microgravity: In space, the absence of gravity (or microgravity) makes it easier to move and assemble large structures that would be impossibly heavy on Earth.

Unlimited Space: The vastness of space offers an unlimited area for expansion, free from terrestrial constraints.

Solar Energy: Abundant and continuous solar energy can be harnessed more efficiently than on Earth, where the atmosphere and day-night cycle limit solar power collection.

Cons:

Extreme Environment: Space is a hostile environment, with extreme temperatures, vacuum, and cosmic radiation posing significant challenges for materials and human safety.

Supply Challenges: All materials and tools must be transported from Earth, a costly and logistically complex endeavor.

Health Risks: Prolonged human presence in space poses health risks, including bone density loss and exposure to radiation.

Vacuum: The vacuum of space is unforgiving. Without proper protection, exposure to space leads to immediate peril from lack of oxygen and extreme temperatures.

Building Underwater: The Abyssal Odyssey
Pros:

Protection from Elements: Underwater structures are shielded from surface weather events like hurricanes and tornadoes.

Abundant Resources: The ocean offers a plethora of resources, including energy (wave, tidal) and potentially untapped minerals and materials. It is teeming with life, from luminescent jellyfish to bizarre creatures like the goblin shark, offering endless opportunities for biological discoveries.

Proximity to Human Civilization: Proximity to land makes transportation of materials and personnel more feasible than space.

Cons:

High Pressure: The immense pressure – over 1,000 times the pressure at sea level – of deep water poses significant engineering challenges, requiring robust and pressure-resistant construction.

Corrosion and Biofouling: Saltwater is corrosive, and marine life can attach to and degrade structures (biofouling).

Limited Sunlight: Sunlight diminishes with depth, limiting the potential for solar power and affecting visibility during construction. It's a realm of near-total darkness, with temperatures often hovering near freezing.

The Unknowns: We have mapped less than 20% of the ocean floor in detail, making each expedition a venture into the unknown, with potential risks of encountering uncharted underwater terrain or unknown geological activity.

The timeless duel between the unfathomable depths of the ocean and the boundless expanse of outer space – two of Earth's final frontiers, each shrouded in mystery and brimming with dangers and wonders alike. Which would you choose?

Congratulations!

You finished! My hope is that something here sparked your curiosity. For those over 40, so much has updated since we left school. Our world is anything but static!

My goal with JJKKGames.com is to keep you connected, keep you thriving. Together.

I retired from teaching as Covid complicated things. Many of my dear old students now have children and complained about the challenges of getting the grandkids and grandparents to engage over video calls during the later lockdowns. Everyone was fatigued.

So I started pulling together bits and bobs that might both interest kids and grandparents, hopefully Mom and Dad too. I send out new books like this often: one for the grandkid, one for the grandparent as a package. It gives them something to lean on if the conversation well dries up. It's been a delightful smash!

Hint, hint: Makes a smart gift for birthdays and holidays.

All of the JJKK Games books are also available in Large Print. For at least 20% off retail, visit me at JJKKGames.com.

It's as if this universe were designed just for us. Let us rejoice!

"In our daily lives, we must see that it is not happiness that makes us grateful, but the gratefulness that makes us happy."
~Albert Clarke

To review sources, please see: JJKKGames.com/sources

What other readers are saying:

"Figured it'd be good for a few lighter moments before uncle starts on about politics. Worked better than expected. (Nephew) ended up sharing so many interesting facts that had talk. Kept (Uncle) quiet. Everyone got involved. Even brothers gf chimed in at one point. Great gift for the curious of all ages."

"(Father-in-law) is not as sharp as he used to be and (my) preteen son has his nose in phone during the supposed quality time. Made for boring zooms which led to fewer ... and as much as i dont miss my ex, we both agree that our son needs his grandpa. So he (the ex) sends these trivia books. Makes for much better zooms. They seem to look forward to talking to each other and i dont have to sit in to keep the conversation going. Its worth it."

Your review is very helpful for other readers and for me making these books better. Please consider leaving a review at your bookstore of choice. Or send me an email through my contact form: jjkkgames.com/comments

Direct link to Amazon review page:

https://www.amazon.com/review/review-your-purchases/listing

Made in the USA
Las Vegas, NV
12 December 2023

82625170R10059